museum new york

a guide

• • •

tanya agathocleus and joseph chaves
photographs by simon alexander

museum new york

a guide

• • • ellipsis

•••

BRITISH LIBRARY CATALOGUING IN PUBLICATION
A CIP record for this book is available from the British Library

PUBLISHED BY •••ellipsis
2 Rufus Street London N1 6PE
EMAIL ...@ellipsis.co.uk
WWW http://www.ellipsis.com
SERIES EDITOR Tom Neville
SERIES DESIGN Jonathan Moberly

COPYRIGHT © 2000 Ellipsis London Limited
ISBN 1 84166 034 5

PRINTING AND BINDING Hong Kong

•••ellipsis is a trademark of Ellipsis
London Limited

For a copy of the Ellipsis catalogue or
information on special quantity orders
of Ellipsis books please contact our sales
manager on 020 7739 3157 or
sales@ellipsis.co.uk

museum new york: a guide

Tanya Agathocleus and Jospeh Chaves 2000

contents

7092 BQI (NEW)

0 introduction
1 lower manhattan
2 village/soho
3 chelsea
4 midtown
5 upper east side
6 upper west side
7 upper manhattan
8 bronx
9 brooklyn
10 queens
11 staten island
12 index

Introduction

Since the nineteenth century, New York's expansive range of important and widely influential museums has played a central role in the constitution of its identity as a world city and as the cultural capital of the USA. Though institutions such as the New York Historical Society and an early version of the Natural History Museum opened as early as 1804 and 1817 respectively, the vast majority of New York's museums were established in the second half of the nineteenth century and the earlier part of the twentieth.

In the wake of the Civil War, the USA changed shape dramatically, increasing in economic prominence on the world stage. Reflecting nationwide migration trends from the country to the city, New York's population expanded from 1 million to 7 million between 1865 and 1930 alone. Its cultural institutions were conceived in large part in response to these significant changes. Museums, libraries, and public spaces like Central Park were seen as means by which the city's increasingly heterogeneous population might be moulded into an educated citizenry. Transforming the Enlightenment ideal of the encyclopedic book into the still more ambitious project of the encyclopedia in a building, museums like the Metropolitan Museum and the Brooklyn Museum defined their goals explicitly as those of educating the public and contributing to the social and moral progress of the nation. Inseparable from the high-minded idealism of museum-builders was the need to consolidate New York's reputation as a cosmopolitan commercial centre comparable to London or Paris. The city's prominent industrialists established their legacies – and shaped the city in the image of their own prosperity – by donating enormous sums of money to New York's nascent museum projects. Railway millionaire Jacob S Rogers, for example, made the Met the richest museum in the world by leaving it $5 million in 1901.

Both the educational roles of nineteenth-century museums and the grandeur they lent to the city, then, were instrumental to the moulding of USA national identity in this period, as the country attempted to match its growing economic rivalry with Europe with competition in the cultural arena. While learned societies like the Numismatic Society flourished, witness to the period's intellectual fervour, the USA's attempts to establish a distinct cultural character through the institutionalisation of aesthetic knowledge were fraught with contradiction from the start. As early as 1826, the founders of the National Academy of Design, highly aware of their inaugural role in establishing a national art-historical tradition, were equally conscious of the European provenance of the very idea of the Academy.

The grandiose turn-of-the-century architecture that housed some of the city's more august museums, heavily influenced by the beaux-arts movement, also imported associations of a grand European cultural heritage into the fledgling cultural scene. Prestigious commissions, particularly those for public buildings, were most likely to be meted out to the more genteel firms whose architects were trained at the École des Beaux Arts in Paris, such as Carrère and Hastings (of Frick and New York Public Library fame) and McKim, Mead & White (designers of the Met and the Brooklyn Museum among many others). In their use of the beaux-arts aesthetic, New York's most influential architects united modern architectural know-how with classical elegance, thus creating buildings that exemplified New York's advantageous position as a cultural link between Old and New World. The New York Public Library, Brooklyn Museum, Audubon Terrace (which houses the Hispanic and Numismatic Societies), the Met and the Museum of Natural History are all continuing legacies of this architectural vision.

Though turn-of-century museums such as the Museum of the City of New York and the Museum of the American Indian modified the ency-clopedic imperatives of earlier museums by training them on local or ethnic cultures, the most significant change in the New York museum landscape came in the 1930s, with the advent of the modern art museum. The Whitney, MoMA, and the Guggenheim, all established within ten years of each other, saw themselves as breaking radically with the past in their devotion to various conceptions of the 'new'. Similarly, the modernist architecture of their buildings revolutionised earlier visions of the cityscape (and subsequently influenced commercial building design in a way that the large-scale ponderousness of the beaux-arts style could never have done).

The later half of the twentieth century has witnessed the New York museum scene build on these late nineteenth- and early twentieth-century legacies substantially. The Museum of Natural History, for example, has recently undertaken extensive renovations in order to mark the enormous shifts in scientific knowledge that have taken place in the last few decades, while the Museum of the American Indian puts the condescending atti-tudes of 19th-century ethnography under scrutiny as part of its exhibi-tions. Furthermore, the kinds of museums open to the public, and the specificity with which they focus on their subject-matter has increased dramatically in recent years. As well as the older museums dedicated to the city of New York, for instance, there are museums devoted to its many different ethnic groups, to its transit system, fire department, municipal archives, and so on. Virtually any cultural phenomenon important to the century has been immortalised in museum form, it seems: pianos, tene-ments and skyscrapers are all preserved as objects of contemplation and interpretation. As much as they have changed shape over the last century, however, New York museums continue to reflect New York's centrality to the cultural life of the USA The city's thriving art scene accounts for the presence of museums like the Dia Center and PS1 – institutions which continue to challenge the parameters of the mainstream art world, now embodied by the once-radical MOMA, Guggenheim and Whitney – while its domination of the media and fashion industries has contributed to the commemoration of these fields in museums such as AMMI, ICP, the Museum of TV and Radio and FIT.

Since World War II, then, the history of New York museums looks less like a linear progression than a flourishing of disparate (or in some cases incommensurate) curatorial goals and imperatives. As a result, the terms of evaluation we used in choosing museums for this book have had to be extremely flexible. The most obvious question we had to ask ourselves – and the one that resulted in the least obvious answers – was 'what is a museum?' Or rather, how are we defining 'museum' for the purposes of inclusion in *Museum New York*? Where does one draw the line between the museum and the gallery, the library, the scholarly institute, and the private collection? In the end, the only prerequisite we adhered to strictly was that a museum is open to the public. Some institutions – especially those for whom the mission of cultural preservation and transmission is more or less self-evident – fulfilled other standard definitions of museums as well: their collections are sizable, of broad appeal, permanent, thoroughly curated, and not for sale.

Many of the institutions we chose to include, however, fit these definitions less squarely. This is especially true of newer museums: some of the most energetic institutions of contemporary art, like PS1, display collections that are not strictly permanent. Instead, they are in large part made up of long-term loans, often from artists directly or indirectly involved in the stewardship of the institution. Similarly, what constitutes an artefact at, say, the Museum of Chinese in the Americas might also be found in a restaurant next door, and may not be recognised as such at, say, the Asia Society. What institutions such as MOCA and PS1 have in common is the questioning or interrogation of the barrier between visiting spectator and curated object – reflective of the fact that the line between museums and other cultural institutions has become less distinct with the passage of time.

We have aspired, like the 19th-century encyclopedic museums, to be comprehensive in our selection of New York museums. However, we make no pretence of being exhaustive. Many of the institutions that occupy the ground between a museum and a gallery have been purposely left for ellipsis' simultaneous publication, *Art New York*. Here, also, are only a sampling of New York's numerous 'house museums', for they are numerous enough almost to make up a book in themselves, and departments in the Brooklyn Museum of Art and the Metropolitan contain sufficient antiquarian furnishings to stock a small village. What we finally included, however, we tried to make a representative sampling, including houses of different styles and functions (federal, early Colonial, farmhouse, hotel-resort) and of different kinds of historical significance (literary, political-historical, nostalgic). Any smaller museums that have eluded our attention, and yet deserve notice, will eventually be reviewed at the ellipsis website, along with those that spring up before the next edition – like the much-anticipated Times Square Sex Museum.

The book is perhaps even less objective than it is exhaustive. However, our purpose is not so much to persuade (still less to prescribe or to circumscribe the museum-goer's experience) as to engage the reader in a conversation which, like any good conversation, makes experience more pleasurable and reflective. We have tried to avoid, at the risk of offending or simply being deemed 'off' in instances, the level, faintly praiseful tone that guidebook writing often invites. Part of our intention is the pragmatic concern that we might help the reader make choices about what to visit: for instance, we want the entry on the Brooklyn Children's Museum to register greater enthusiasm than that for the Manhattan Children's Museum.

Our sense of what's worth visiting in New York has changed dramatically over the course of writing this book. Some of the institutions that were once lowest on our personal lists of places to visit (like the Museum of American Folk Art, the Fire Museum, and the American Numismatic Society) turned out to be among the most enjoyable and enlightening, and we want to convey that to the reader.

Moreover, the book contains evaluative judgments that we hope are useful, if not authoritative. You may not find PS1 so challenging, the National Academy of Design so inconsequential, or the Forbes Magazine Galleries so weirdly compelling as we did. We hope, though, to have expressed such assessments judiciously and eloquently enough that they are not reducible to mere opining, and so that they give the reader something to chew on and/or spit out. In entries that are modestly critical of a given museum, we have also attempted to describe faithfully the institution's sense of its own mission. While this is not a series of position papers, then, recent and not-so-recent debates about the function of the museum loosely inform the book. We have aimed for a blend of historical context, critical analysis and synthetic description in our writing: this is not infospeak, but you can still digest it on the Z train between the museum of X and the Y society – it's a user's guide.

museum new york: a guide

Using this book

New York is made up of five boroughs: Manhattan, the Bronx, Brooklyn, Queens and Staten Island. Since Manhattan is by far the most populous museum-wise, we have divided it into Upper Manhattan (above 125th Street), Upper West Side, Upper East Side, Midtown, Chelsea, Village/Soho and Lower Manhattan (below Canal). We created these areas by taking existing neighbourhood divisions and adapting them slightly to match museum demographics so that each 'neighbourhood' we've created contains a sufficient number of museums, and visits of several institutions at once can be planned accordingly. Within most of these geographical divisions, (except for Upper Manhattan, Staten Island and Queens because of their size) it is fairly easy to get from one museum to another (either by subway, bus or on foot). The relatively small size of the neighbourhoods below 14th Street makes them particularly walkable, and Lower Manhattan, though horribly crowded during rush-hour and weekday lunchtime, has some of the most stunning architecture in the city, so is well worth traversing by foot.

New York museums in general are most quickly and inexpensively visited by subway. Therefore subway stops are listed for each museum, but most, of course, are also accessible by bus and car – visit museum websites or 'phone to get directions if you prefer these modes of transport. Ask for free subway maps at subway toll booths: a map book such as *Flashmaps New York* (available at most bookstores and some newsstands) is also helpful in negotiating the city, especially Downtown, where numbered streets are replaced by named ones and the New York grid ceases to seem logical.

Refillable subway Metrocards of various denominations and one-ride tokens ($1.50) can be purchased at booths or at the automated machines next to them. If you're in New York for longer than an afternoon, it makes sense to buy a Metrocard of at least $15, as you get one free ride for every $15 you put on the card.

For further information on New York museums, we find the *NYC Culture Catalog* to be one of the best and most comprehensive guides to city sites and museums. It's also worth looking up the museum sections on New York City-related websites, such as cityinsights.com, newyorknet.com or newyork.citysearch.com. The websites that we list in each museum's entry are extremely useful as well, and often offer up-to-the-minute information on holiday closing times and special exhibitions that are worth checking before your visit.

lower manhattan

Ellis Island Immigration Museum **1.2**
Fraunces Tavern Museum **1.6**
Lower East Side Tenement Museum **1.10**
Municipal Archives of the City of New York **1.14**
Museum of Chinese in the Americas (MoCA) **1.16**
Museum of Jewish Heritage **1.20**
National Museum of the American Indian **1.24**
Museum of the American Piano **1.28**
The Skyscraper Museum **1.30**
South Street Seaport Museum **1.32**

Ellis Island Immigration Museum

Set aside a few hours for this dramatic museum experience. While getting there can be something of an ordeal (take the boat from Battery Park City), there are impressive views of the downtown skyline along the way, and the museum itself is well worth the trip. A timely counter to a growing wave of anti-immigration legislation in recent years, the museum opened in 1990 to study and celebrate the Ellis Island immigration experience and its formative relationship to national history. It is estimated that almost half of the country's population can trace their ancestry back to immigrants who passed through Ellis Island.

The museum is designed to replicate the various stages of an immigrant's journey to America, from the boat trip itself through each step of the bureaucratic process. Though this concept could have produced an annoyingly contrived experience, it actually works well in practice, thanks to the careful balance between historical detail and individual narrative in each of the displays. Focusing on the key years 1880 to 1925, when immigration to Ellis Island was at its height, the museum records the immigration process down to the minutest detail – from physical and psychological testing to legal inspection and money exchange – along with the historical imperatives that dictated these procedures. For instance, an intriguing display of political cartoons depicts the shifting national opinions that defined immigration policy over the three decades the museum was in operation.

Large parts of the exhibition tell the immigration story through personal recollections, suggesting that the immigrant experience cannot be captured as a totality, but only as the disparate experiences of individuals with vastly different ethnic and religious backgrounds. Larger-than-life photographs of past immigrants stare down at you from the walls, recorded oral histories are placed strategically around the exhibits,

and quotations from people remembering their immigration experience supplement all the more general historical information. Even the incidental materials of the experience are brought to the visitor's attention. Reconstructed dormitory rooms with tiny hanging cots are on view, as is graffiti preserved on slabs on concrete, while objects once meaningful to the travellers who brought them, such as clothing, religious items and personal papers, are displayed with reverence. The museum's thoughtful approach to the subject-matter extends beyond its main exhibition to the displays about immigrant life after Ellis Island: topics such as work, religion, art, assimilation and naturalisation are explored in depth.

On the bottom floor, inventive three-dimensional graphs and charts help visitors to visualise the enormous shifts in population that marked migratory trends, like the slave trade and the turn-of-the-century immigration explosion. Self-guided audio-tours are available in many languages and a research library and oral-history listening room are open to the public. Visitors are invited to involve themselves in the museum's project of documenting diversity by contributing their names and portraits to the American Family Album: they can also add their own immigration histories to the Family Research database.

ADDRESS New York Harbor, New York, NY 10004; (212) 363 3200; www.ellisisland.org
OPEN daily, 9.00–17.00
ADMISSION $7 (includes ferry fare)
DISABILITY ACCESS full
SUBWAY 1, 9 to South Ferry; N, R to Whitehall; 4, 5 to Bowling Green; then take ferry to Ellis Island

Fraunces Tavern Museum

Still a functioning eating establishment popular with Wall Street power-lunchers, Fraunces Tavern serves as a bridge between New York's early colonial history and its current incarnation as a centre of world finance. Nestled demurely among some of New York's tallest skyscrapers, the structure looks much the way it did in 1719, when it was built as a mansion for a prosperous merchant, Stephen Delancey. Though the building was remodelled over the years, interest in the Revolutionary period revived at the turn of the century, prompting an early preservation effort. Finally, in 1904, it was restored to its original appearance. Though the building served several different functions over the years (including host to government departments when New York was the nation's first capital) it probably saw its most eventful years when it was owned by Samuel Fraunces, from 1762 to 1785.

An intriguing, ambitious character, thought to have once served as a spy for George Washington, Fraunces turned the erstwhile mansion into a popular and prestigious tavern, where both raucous entertainment and radical political activity thrived. The museum, located on the first and second floors of the building, manages to pack a good amount of information about these events into a series of small exhibitions and installations. For instance, you learn that the New York Tea Party was launched from the tavern in 1774, and in 1783 George Washington hosted a farewell dinner for the officers of the Continental Army in the tavern's Long Room, an event that the museum has immortalised by reconstructing the room as it may have looked on the night, complete with place settings and fake roast chicken. The Clinton Room displays an early 19th century dining room: be sure to check out the elaborate but shamelessly inaccurate panoramic wallpaper, depicting Revolutionary war events taking place against a lavish Hudson Valley landscape. The museum also offers

Fraunces Tavern Museum

changing exhibitions on early American history and culture, an interesting selection of school and public programmes, evening lectures, family-oriented workshops and Colonial and Revolutionary New York walking tours. The restaurant and bar areas, located on the ground floor of the building, are run separately and are open on weekdays for dining. (Don't expect Colonial fare, though, the menu is standard American.) The dark, dust-filmed appearance of the dining rooms, which might be offputting in a different restaurant, manages to enhance the Colonial tavern atmosphere that the restaurant is trying to recreate.

ADDRESS 54 Pearl Street (corner of Pearl and Broad Streets) New York, NY 10004; (212) 425 1778
OPEN Monday to Friday, 10.00–16.45; Saturday, 12.00–16.00
ADMISSION $2.50; seniors, students and children, $1; children under six, free
DISABILITY ACCESS none
SUBWAY 1, 9 to South Ferry; 2, 3 to Wall Street; 4, 5 to Bowling Green; N, R to Whitehall

Lower East Side Tenement Museum

The Tenement Museum, founded by Ruth Abram in 1988, is dedicated to preserving and interpreting the history of working class immigrants at the turn of the century. It boasts an excellent website: among other well-designed features, visitors can see eleven different 'doll's-house dioramas' that present fictionalised moments from the lives of immigrant families who are known to have lived in the museum's tenement building. The museum's prize exhibit, the tenement at 97 Orchard Street (located across the street from the visitor centre and gift shop) is interactive in the old-fashioned sense, however: it is a preserved 19th-century tenement building that visitors are invited to explore with the help of its knowledgeable tour guides. Discovered boarded up since 1935 by the museum's founders, the tenement was a rare 'time capsule' find, as most remaining New York tenements have been radically overhauled or rebuilt to comply with housing laws.

The building has been preserved more or less in its original state with minimal restoration – though selected items of furniture and period wallpaper, for example, are new additions. Excessively dim lighting underscores the fact that for much of the building's history its inhabitants endured lack of light, heat, and running water. Visitors are led into dusty, uneven, incredibly cramped rooms and told the stories of their original inhabitants. You are asked to imagine the life of Nathalie Gumpertz, a dressmaker who supported her four children on her own after her husband disappeared from the building in 1874. Standing in the 325-square-foot apartment where she spent her childhood, you hear the voice of Josephine Baldizzi, captured on tape as oral history, reminiscing about trips to the local Nickelodeon theatre in the 1930s. Rather than romanticising these singular lives, however, the museum attempts to situate each individual story within the history of the neighbourhood and the cultural

Lower East Side Tenement Museum

heritage that immigrants brought with them. Deeply committed to the neighbourhood it commemorates, the museum also reminds visitors that many of the Lower East Side's adverse conditions, including sweatshops, continue to prevail in the surrounding streets. The museum's programmes and special events are as thoughtfully executed as its main exhibit, and include walking tours of the neighbourhood, art exhibitions and children's parties. Its annual Halloween programme, Hallowed Halls, is both critically acclaimed and hugely popular. Featuring site-specific installations by different artists who take up temporary residence in nooks of the tenement's unrestored rooms, the event uses the unsettling atmosphere of Halloween as an occasion to explore various aspects of the building's history.

ADDRESS 90 Orchard Street (corner of Broome Street), New York, NY 10002; (212) 431-0233; www.tenement.org
OPEN Tuesday to Friday, 12.00–17.00 (extended to 19.00 on Thursday, April to October); Saturday, Sunday, 11.00–17.00; tours at 13.00, 14.00, 15.00 and 16.00 on weekdays and every 30 minutes at weekends
ADMISSION $9; students and seniors, $7
DISABILITY ACCESS none
SUBWAY F, J to Delancey

Municipal Archives of the City of New York

The archives are a gargantuan collection of New York's bureaucratic documents – building and planning records, films, genealogical records, maps, census statistics, and photographs. The artefacts available in the public reference room include plans for the original construction of the Brooklyn Bridge in 1867, manuscripts and photographs from the depression era WPA Federal Writers' Project, photographs of every building in the five boroughs for the period 1939-41 (amassed by the Department of Taxes for the purposes of property appraisal), and District Attorney's case files going back to the end of the 18th century. Copies of this material can be requested: you can order personal birth, death, and marriage certificates on-line.

You will have to wander confusedly through the building's gorgeous lobby to find the reference room, and then wait for someone to lead you down to the display of the permanent collections. Documents displayed range from the quirky to the historically important. When I visited, it included an invoice to the city from its Public Whipper, a 1945 Christmas card to the mayor of New York from the US Forces' War Crimes Investigation Team, and the purchase agreement between Indians and the Dutch for the 'Island of the Manhattans'.

ADDRESS Department of Records and Information Services, 31 Chambers Street, Room 103 (at City Hall Park), New York, NY 10007; (212) 788 8580; www.ci.nyc.ny.us/html/doris/home.html
OPEN Monday to Thursday, 9.00–16.30; Friday, 9.00–13.00
ADMISSION free
DISABILITY ACCESS full
SUBWAY 4, 5, 6 to Brooklyn Bridge

lower manhattan

Museum of Chinese in the Americas (MoCA)

Located in Chinatown in a huge century-old ex-schoolhouse, MoCA is unique in its mission to preserve and exhibit the Chinese immigration experience and Chinese-American history. It sees itself less as an institution of high culture than as one among a number of community-outreach programmes that have taken up residence in the building. A placard in one of the museum's displays invites visitors to listen to strains of singing from the floor below where daily Cantonese opera performances take place, while flyers about neighbourhood cultural and social events line the museum's entry-hall.

The enterprise began life as the 'Chinatown History Project' in 1980, when a group of activists and intellectuals decided to record the swiftly changing history of the neighbourhood, heretofore consigned to obscurity. Eventually the project grew in scope, as its curators came to see the history of Chinatown as inseparable from the larger, continuing migration history of the Chinese in the Americas. Hence, while the museum focuses on local history, its exhibits gesture outwards to other cities and USA history more generally.

A tiny but entrancing museum, MoCA consist of only two rooms. One, shaped like a lantern, houses the permanent exhibition and has the eclectic, vibrant look of a Chinatown general store: another small room hosts temporary installations and exhibitions.

Paradoxically but intriguingly, the permanent collection is devoted to transience: everyday material objects, some found on the street and in skips, are displayed as relics of the immigrants that once used them and as fleeting sources of meaning and identity. One display on Chinese businesses proffers menus, matchbooks and other restaurant paraphernalia, while another showcases the changing tools of the laundry trade. While

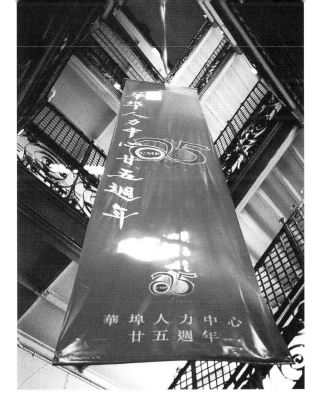

lower manhattan

the museum's diminutive size could make this collection seem reductive of its immense subject, the exhibition's signage encourages visitors to see its reconstruction of history as partial and continuing. Entitled 'Where is Home?', it asks visitors to engage dynamically with the objects and histories on display, contributing their own stories and thoughts in writing (whether or not they're Chinese), and solicits the donation of artefacts and ideas.

In keeping with the ideal of a collection in dialogue with its public, the museum hosts a variety of cultural and community events – such as reunions, readings, and art exhibitions – that invite members of the community to exchange and contribute oral histories. Thanks to these and earlier efforts, MOCA also has an extensive archive of primary resource material on Chinese-American history and culture that includes sound recordings and textiles.

ADDRESS 2nd floor, 70 Mulberry Street (at Bayard Street), New York, NY 10013; (212) 619 4785; www.MoCA-nyc.org
OPEN Tuesday to Saturday, 12.00–17.00
ADMISSION (suggested) $3; seniors and students $1; children under 12 free
DISABILITY ACCESS none
SUBWAY N, R, J, M or 6 to Canal Street; B, D, Q to Grand Street

Museum of Jewish Heritage

Established in 1977 in a distinctive hexagonal building at the tip of the attractive, newly landscaped riverfront of Battery Place, the Museum of Jewish Heritage – A Living Memorial to the Holocaust (its full name) has much more packed within its walls than the diminutive appearance of the building might lead one to expect. The museum strives to both acknowledge and transcend the horrors of the Holocaust by setting itself up as a historical journey towards, through, and away from it. The ground floor illustrates pre-war Jewish life in Europe and North Africa through the display of religious and cultural artefacts, such as a hand-painted sukkah canvas from Budapest. An innovative multimedia presentation that overlays different ways of conceptualising Jewish identity supplements the more traditional archival material.

Most compelling and impressively curated, however, is the first floor, dedicated to the Holocaust. There, dark lighting, a strangely contorted gallery space and a cacophony of voices in distress playing on tape set the stage for a devastating experience of historical witnessing. Like the more famous Holocaust Museum in DC, this one focuses on individual histories in order to tell an overwhelmingly large story, and the walls and walls of photographs, possessions and narratives relating to concentration-camp victims and survivors combine to gut-wrenching effect.

The bright lights and colours of the top floor, devoted to 'Jewish Renewal', provide an optimistic, though somewhat jarring counterpoint. The exhibition itself focuses on the founding and growth of Israel, and Jewish contributions to American life, while a hallway with a view of the river and the Statue of Liberty invites the visitor to view as commensurate the progressive narratives of Jewish renewal and immigration to the USA.

The museum offers several family-oriented programmes, including

Museum of Jewish Heritage

weekly Sunday activities that explore the significance of Jewish customs and holidays through craft workshops, music, and story-telling. Another of its resources, the Bess Myerson Film and Video Collection, makes documentaries and feature films with Jewish themes available to educators and students: in addition, frequent film screenings are open to the public, and the museum has begun to sponsor film festivals as well.

ADDRESS 18 First Place, Battery Park City, New York, NY 10004; (212) 509 6130; www.mjhnyc.org
OPEN Sunday to Wednesday, 9.00–17.00; Thursday, 9.00–20.00; Friday (and eve of Jewish holidays), 9.00–15.00; summer Fridays, 9.00–17.00
ADMISSION $7; seniors and students $5; children of five and under free
DISABILITY ACCESS full (wheelchairs and care chairs available)
SUBWAY 1, 9 to South Ferry; 4, 5 to Bowling Green; A, C, E to World Trade Center

National Museum of the American Indian

Designed by Cass Gilbert in 1899, the Alexander Hamilton US Custom House, with its grandiose marble, mural-laden interior and glass-domed rotunda, is a monument to Gilded Age hubris. At its entrance, one of four stone statues is meant to represent America. Her foot rests on the head of the Aztec god Quetzalcoatl, while behind her a lone Indian figure stands surrounded by shattered fragments of Native art. By taking up residence within this dramatic Beaux Arts building, the National Museum of the American Indian casts an ironic light on the statue's stereotype of Indian culture as vanquished and vanishing. Created by a 1989 Act of Congress to celebrate the historical and contemporary culture of Native peoples across the Americas, the museum represents approximately 600 Indian nations and is staffed by Native Americans from a variety of these. Over a million objects from throughout the Americas are held in its collection, which spans a period of 10,000 years and includes Mexican and Peruvian textiles, Navajo weaving, garments from the North American plains Indians, and Aztec mosaics. The New York branch of the museum (there are eventually to be divisions in DC and Maryland as well) is officially known as the George Gustav Haye Center, after the New York banker who started the collection in 1903. In 1990, the museum moved from its uptown location to the Custom House and became part of the Smithsonian.

The museum's original ethnographic mandate has changed considerably over the years: in its new incarnation, it has a repatriation programme that returns illegally acquired objects to Indian tribes or individuals on demand. Using innovative curatorial methods, the museum strives to combat past misrepresentations of Native art and to affirm Native contexts and beliefs. Some displays, for example, are inter-

lower manhattan

1.26

lower manhattan

preted by not one but many placards, each offering a different reading of the piece on view. Placed side by side, the contrasting archaeological, anthropological and Native analyses demonstrate to visitors the many contexts in which the objects on display could be understood. While the idea of producing multiple perspectives for art that has historically been viewed reductively is a salutary gesture, it proves difficult to execute elegantly. The amount of information presented, together with the vast range of time and space covered, can be so disorienting that in some displays the context seems to disappear altogether. Despite the busyness of text and ideas, however, the exhibition's visual presentation of exquisite examples of textiles, art and artefacts is skilfully spare. The museum also has an impressive photographic archive, a film and video centre that holds frequent screenings, and a number of good web- and CD-ROM-based resources.

ADDRESS One Bowling Green, New York, NY 10004; (212) 514 3799; www.si.edu/nmai/
OPEN Monday to Sunday, 10.00–17.00
ADMISSION free
DISABILITY ACCESS full
SUBWAY 4, 5 to Bowling Green; N, R to Whitehall Street

Museum of the American Piano

This minuscule museum will be of particular interest to piano buffs and those interested in the history of music, but the simplicity of its dedication to a single instrument can make it a satisfying experience even for those only tangentially interested in keyboard culture. The museum was founded by Kalman Detrich. A talented restorer of antique pianos, Detrich collects instruments of historical, technical or musical significance, restores them to their original playing condition and makes them available to the public through their display in the museum. Above each piano on display is posted information about its maker, the composers who wrote for this version of the instrument, and the kind of compositions habitually played on it.

The museum's distinctiveness stems from the fact that you can interact with these delicate instruments in a way you could not at, say, the Met. Detrich's courses and lectures not only teach the history of early instruments and keyboards, but also more hands-on skills, such as piano-tuning and technology. At some of these venues, music students are encouraged to try out early versions of the piano for themselves: more importantly, at least for the layperson, the recitals offer the opportunity to listen to the different sonorities and capabilities of each instrument.

ADDRESS 291 Broadway, New York, NY 10019; (212) 246 4646; www.pianomuseum.com
OPEN for lectures and recitals with advance reservation
ADMISSION $15
DISABILITY ACCESS yes
SUBWAY A, C to Chambers Street; N, R to City Hall

MUSEUM OF THE AMERICAN PIANO
211 W. 58th ST. N.Y., N.Y
212/246-4646

American Piano Museum
Is moving to new
location.

lower manhattan

The Skyscraper Museum

The museum's definition of a skyscraper – a building that is 'taller than square' – allows for the fact that a building's size, and hence skyscraper status, is usually relative to the size of those around it. Founded in 1996, the museum compiles and presents skyscraper history in relation to the evolution of business cycles and the economic history of the urban development. In a recent exhibition on the making of the Empire State Building, the relationship between finance and architectural form is neatly brought to the visitor's attention through the fact that photographs of the building under construction are mounted in former teller windows.

The museum's exhibits generally include a wide range of materials and artefacts relating to skyscraper history, including architectural models, construction photographs, blueprints, real-estate documents, contractors' notebooks, film and newspaper articles. Though these materials can feel a little dry when compared to the dramatic reality of the skylines they document, the museum's archival work is impressive in scale and accessible in format, particularly as it is now available through the Virtual Archive on the museum's well-designed website. The museum also sponsors lectures, educational programmes, walking tours and publications. As of fall 2001, the Skyscraper Museum will move to Battery Park City (in a building opposite the Museum of Jewish Heritage).

ADDRESS 110 Maiden Lane, New York; (212) 968 1961; www.skyscraper.org.
OPEN Tuesday to Saturday, 12.00–18.00
ADMISSION (suggested) $2
DISABILITY ACCESS full (telephone in advance)
SUBWAY 4, 5 or 2, 3 to Wall Street

South Street Seaport Museum

This is a monument to a neighbourhood and to several centuries of New York's port life. The exhibits are spread out over a 12-square-block historical district amid upmarket shops, Fulton Fish Market, and attractive historic buildings. Exhibits document every facet of local maritime life, including labour, immigration, leisure, commerce, disasters, and even the role of ports in making New York the literary capital of the USA in the 19th century. The permanent collection contains nearly 10,000 artefacts, including sailors' gear, ship fittings, shipboard tools, and works of art.

Start at the visitors' centre at 12–14 Fulton Street and pick up a map. Then to the 'Norway Galleries', or to the Children's Center. Next to the printing shop are the Whitman Gallery (focusing on ship models and ocean liner memorabilia) and the temporary exhibits of the Melville Gallery. Six historic ships in the harbour have restored staterooms and sailing equipment. These can be toured, and one of them takes visitors on excursions into the harbour. At Water Street is New York Unearthed, South Street Seaport's museum of New York archaeology.

Many of the programmes at the museum are aimed at children and are mostly highly interactive. The activities for adults include volunteer preservation projects, and even international sailing trips. The museum also plays host to photographic exhibitions, concerts, and lectures.

ADDRESS Visitors' Center, 12–14 Fulton Street, New York, NY 10038; (212) 748 8600; www.southstseaport.org
OPEN Monday to Sunday, 10.00–18.00
ADMISSION $6; seniors $5; students $4; children $3
DISABILITY ACCESS limited
SUBWAY 2, 3, 4, 5, J, M, Z to Fulton Street; A, C to Broadway/Nassau Street; E to World Trade Center

lower manhattan

village/soho

Forbes Magazine Galleries 2.2
Merchant's House Museum 2.4
Museum for African Art 2.8
New York City Fire Museum 2.12
The Ukrainian Museum 2.14

Forbes Magazine Galleries

At first glance, this museum of collectibles in the lobby of the Forbes Magazine building looks like an afterthought. A closer look reveals an intriguingly idiosyncratic collection. Though their chief attractions are the famous Fabergé eggs, the galleries are equally interesting as a display of the family's private obsessions, which include toy soldiers, boats and strange historical artefacts. In owning and displaying the eggs – treasures from the end of the Romanov dynasty – along with handcrafted toys and other souvenirs of a leisured past, the Forbeses seem to be trying to recapture the glamour and self-importance of aristocratic art patronage, albeit with a healthy dose of self-consciousness: an exhibition of Monopoly boards, for instance, bears the slogan 'How I Became a Capitalist'.

Historical trivia such as Theodore Roosevelt's note to his son's teacher, asking if the boy could be excused due to election excitement, are displayed alongside more significant documents such as Lincoln's last public address and a copy of the Emancipation Proclamation. Beyond this room, the collection gets truly weird. One of the toy galleries' more surreal offerings, the 'Land of Counterpane', involves sticking your head into a glass bubble so that you can see yourself (with the aid of a mirror) as a boy in his bedroom surrounded by toy soldiers – an instance of the Forbes placing visitors inside their private fantasies. A more sedate fine art gallery contains American and nineteenth-century European paintings.

ADDRESS Forbes Building, 62 Fifth Avenue (at 12th Street) New York, NY 10011; (212) 206 5548
OPEN Tuesday, Wednesday, Friday, Saturday, 10.00–16.00
ADMISSION free
DISABILITY ACCESS full
SUBWAY 4, 5, 6, N, R, L to Union Square

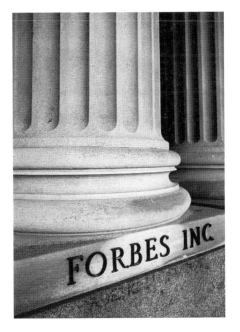

Merchant's House Museum

Unobtrusively situated on a brownstone street in Greenwich Village, this museum merits a pause in your downtown day, particularly if you're interested in an instant evocation of the New York of Henry James' Washington Square. The city's only nineteenth-century family home that has been preserved intact and is open to the public, it was built as a row house in 1832, in the then popular Greek Revival style. Home to a wealthy merchant with the improbably Dickensian name, Seabury Tredwell, and his large family (he had eight children in all), the house remained in the family for almost a century. Even as the neighbourhood became progressively less fashionable, and uptown addresses began to replace downtown ones among the city's elite families, the Tredwells stayed on – Gertrude Tredwell eventually died in the house in 1933, and it was turned into a museum shortly thereafter. Neither its interior nor its exterior are much changed from their original state. Opulent rooms on the ground and first floor are stocked with the house's original designer furniture (including pieces by nineteenth-century New York's illustrious cabinet-makers, Duncan Phyfe and Joseph Meeks), marble mantelpieces, Argand oil lamps and period clothing. The parlour is particularly noteworthy as an example of the relentless symmetry of the Greek Revival style: fake 'pocket doors' were put in to mirror those that actually led to other rooms. Also of interest are the modern conveniences that the Tredwells were among the first to possess, including piping for gas, a 4000-gallon cistern, and a bell system for summoning the house's four live-in servants.

The tour's commentary is as interesting for what it cannot tell you about the gender of the house's erstwhile occupants as for what it can. For instance, because both boys and girls were dressed in skirts and pantelettes, the museum is unable to identify the sex of the child in the portrait in the dining room. Similarly, neither Mr nor Mrs Tredwell's

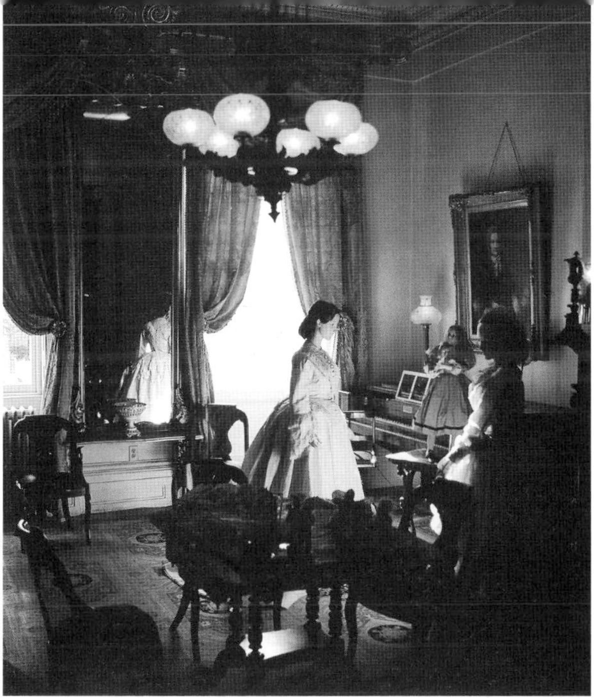

bedrooms left curators much evidence about which of the pair occupied which room. If you're there in the spring or summer, be sure to visit the garden, which has been reconstructed in period style and feels incongruously delicate next to the large buildings that now hover around it. The museum hosts a number of educational programmes, including walking tours of historic buildings, lectures, concerts, readings and annual fundraising celebrations, such as the New York City Oyster Festival. Its small gift shop also doubles as a charity shop, where donated items, such as china and glassware, are sold to benefit the museum.

ADDRESS 29 East Fourth Street (between Lafayette and Bowery), New York, NY 10003; (212) 777 1089; www.merchantshouse.com
OPEN Monday to Thursday, 13.00–17.00
ADMISSION $5; students and seniors $3; children under 12 free
DISABILITY ACCESS none
SUBWAY N, R to Eighth Street; 6 to Astor Place; D, F to Broadway/Lafayette

Museum for African Art

As one of only two major museums in the USA dedicated exclusively to historical and contemporary African art and culture, this museum has played a major role in changing both institutional and popular attitudes towards its subject matter. In an effort to revise the traditional Western view of African art as curio or anthropological artefact, the curators tend to strike a balance between explaining the original context for the art (or lack thereof, as much of its history was lost or distorted during the slave trade and colonial period), and celebrating its aesthetic function.

Though the museum is fairly small, its exhibits rarely feel trivial or cramped, thanks to the museum's well-proportioned, skilfully lighted rooms, designed by Vietnam Veterans' Memorial architect Maya Lin. A combination of traditional African materials and colours with modern Western gallery space, Lin's design provides a stable frame for the radical restructuring that accommodates each new exhibition. Shows, which typically take over the whole museum, tend to explore broad but interesting and eclectic themes, ranging from 1993's travelling exhibition 'To Cure and Protect: Sickness and Health in African Art' and the recent 'Liberated Voices: Contemporary Art from South Africa' to 2000's 'Status, Symbol and Style: Hair in African Art and Culture'.

The museum showcases a wide variety of media, including painting, sculptures, installations, photographs, and videos. Although it does not as yet have a permanent exhibition, its impressive gift shop, spread over the spacious front room of the museum, practically functions as one: the textiles, decorative pieces and jewellery that stock the shop are displayed as museum pieces in their own right, complete with signage that details their origins and the processes of their creation. Here again, a diversity of media is represented, including cloth, metal, wood, ceramic, straw, leather, gourd, and plastic. Some of the pieces on sale are specially

commissioned by the museum. The shop also stocks an excellent collection of books on African art, published by the museum's own critically acclaimed publishing programme. An impressive series of public programmes includes hands-on artmaking workshops for children, lectures for adults, and music and theatrical performances for both. The museum also organises group art tours to architecture and art destinations in Africa, Portugal and Spain.

ADDRESS 593 Broadway (between Houston and Prince), New York, NY 10012; (212) 966-1313; www.africanart.org
OPEN Tuesday to Friday, 10.30–17.30; Saturday, Sunday, 12.00–18.00
ADMISSION $5; seniors, students and children $2.50
DISABILITY ACCESS full
SUBWAY N, R to Prince Street; B, D, Q, F to Broadway/Lafayette

New York City Fire Museum

An unexpectedly rewarding museum experience, even for adults, the Fire Museum – located just on the edge of Soho in an imposing 1904 firehouse – offers a vivid evocation of firefighting over the last two centuries. The collection ranges from fire insurance marks, antique helmets, and gorgeously detailed hand- and horse-drawn early fire engines in pristine condition, to toys and models of fire equipment, and photographs of firefighting incidents. The museum also documents changing representations of firefighters and the fire department. While some of the 'fire-related art' that it advertises is less than fascinating and not a little kitsch, most of it is at least of historical interest, particularly the nineteenth-century cartoons.

The Fire Safety Education Program is one of the Museum's more explicit attempts to function as a public service. Run by friendly active and retired firefighters, the programme teaches school groups about fire safety and then puts them through their paces in a simulated emergency situation. Students enter a darkened mock apartment, rigged with black lights to highlight a range of potential fire hazards. When a fire alarm goes off, they have to make their way through clouds of smoke to the exit using their newly acquired fire safety skills: a scary but effective (and no doubt fun) little lesson. The museum also caters firefighting-themed birthday parties for kids aged 4 through 8.

ADDRESS 278 Spring Street (between Hudson and Varick), New York, NY 10013; (212) 691 1303; www.nycfiremuseum.org
OPEN Tuesday to Sunday, 10.00–16.00
ADMISSION $4; seniors and students $2; children under 12, $1
DISABILITY ACCESS full
SUBWAY 1, 9 to Houston Street; C, E to Spring Street

The Ukrainian Museum

In step with many of the museums of ethnic or regional orientation in New York, the Ukrainian Museum aspires to represent all facets of Ukrainian life, but places a special emphasis on immigration to the USA. Indeed, a good many of the artefacts on display literally came out of the trunks of early twentieth-century immigrants to the museum's neighbourhood. While rising rents have driven many Eastern Europeans elsewhere, their presence in the East Village persists through the museum, and in neighbouring restaurants and churches.

On the top floor, long-term exhibitions of the folk art collection display a range of textiles, jewellery, dolls, decorative objects, and an outstanding collection of colourful Ukrainian Easter eggs, or *pysanky*. The wedding and festive attire is particularly attractive. On the floor below, the fine arts exhibition rotates more rapidly, and often displays objects on loan. The permanent collection includes drawings, paintings, and sculptures made in the Ukraine, and by artists of Ukrainian descent working in Europe and the USA. The fine arts collection focuses on the twentieth century and represents artists of widely varied quality and stature, ranging from Alexander Archipenko to relative unknowns. Less often shown is the significant archival collection, which documents immigration to the USA, as well as Ukrainian architecture and dress. The museum also sponsors public programmes and an impressive array of bilingual publications.

ADDRESS 203 2nd Avenue, New York, NY 10003; (212) 228 0110; www.brama.com/ukrainian_museum
OPEN Wednesday to Sunday, 13.00–17.00
ADMISSION $3; seniors and students $2; children under 12 free
DISABILITY ACCESS full
SUBWAY 6 to Astor Place; N, R to 8th Street; L to 1st Avenue

chelsea

Dia Center for the Arts **3.2**
The Museum at Fashion Institute of Technology **3.6**

Dia Center for the Arts

From Joseph Beuys' *7000 Oaks*, which lines the sidewalk in front of the building, to Dan Graham's *Rooftop Urban Park Project*, the Dia Center's focus on commissioning large-scale, continuing, and even multi-site projects is evident. *7000 Oaks* consists of several trees, each accompanied by a piece of basalt, and is part of a project whose other site is the entire town of Kassel, Germany. Next to the extremely pleasant rooftop café, the two-way mirrored glass of Graham's open-air pavilion becomes either transparent or reflective, depending on the movement of viewers, the surrounding cityscape, and atmospheric conditions.

The Dia Center was founded in 1974, but opened its West 22nd Street exhibition space in 1987. In the late 1970s and early 1980s, the museum's acquisitions focused on American and German art of the 1960s and 1970s, and was remarkably attuned to the art of those decades that would have lasting resonance: acquisitions included works by artists such as Joseph Beuys, Dan Flavin, Barnett Newman, Blinky Palermo, Cy Twombly, and Andy Warhol. The choice of works commissioned during the 1980s (by artists including Robert Ryman, Francesco Clemente, Jenny Holzer, Brice Marden, and Lawrence Weiner) have by now shown equal foresight.

A great part of the appeal for both artists and visitors has been Dia's willingness to put on shows on a mammoth scale, such as Gerhard Richter's 1996 Atlas. Since 1995, in keeping with its demonstrated prescience, the Dia Center has supported several digital media projects. In addition to basic information, the extensive website contains videos of installations, essays on the artworks, and information on the funding of each project.

The Dia Center also displays pieces at other locations, such as Walter De Maria's *New York Earth Room*, a 3500-square-foot room filled with

soil to a depth of 22 inches (on permanent exhibition at 141 Wooster Street), and site-specific works in Texas and New Mexico.

Potential visitors to the Dia Center should note that it closes for a good part of each summer.

ADDRESS 548 West 22nd Street (off Eleventh Avenue), New York, NY 10011; (212) 989 5566; www.diacenter.org
OPEN Wednesday to Sunday, 12.00–18.00 (closed June to August)
ADMISSION adults $6; students and seniors $3
DISABILITY ACCESS full
SUBWAY A, C, E to 23rd Street

The Museum at Fashion Institute of Technology

One of the world's largest collection of costumes, textiles, and accessories, the Museum at FIT holds apparel from as far back as the eighteenth century, but strongly emphasises dress of the twentieth century. Its collection of textiles, swatches and sample books numbers in the hundreds of thousands.

While the immediate audience for the temporary shows consists of the students of the Institute, the Museum at FIT seeks to appeal to fashion writers, historians, and casual observers of *la mode*. Exhibitions of work by students, faculty, and unaffiliated designers vary widely both in topic and quality. Those that display works verging on conceptual art tend to be less impressive than the exhibitions that explore the business and technology of fashion and interior design, or those that present retrospectives of the work of major designers. As well as maintaining the collection, the museum's conservation department performs research in the fields of textile and costume conservation.

ADDRESS Seventh Avenue (at 27th Street), New York, NY 10001; (212) 217 5970 (information 217 5800); www.fitnyc.suny.edu
OPEN Tuesday to Friday, 12.00–20.00; Saturday, 10.00–17.00
ADMISSION free
DISABILITY ACCESS full
SUBWAY 1, 9 to 27th St.; A, E, F to 23rd Street

chelsea

midtown

American Craft Museum 4.2
Americas Society 4.4
Intrepid Sea Air Space Museum 4.6
Japan Society 4.10
The Morgan Library 4.12
The Museum of Modern Art (MoMA) 4.16
Museum of TV & Radio 4.20
Newseum/NY 4.24
The New York Public Library 4.26
United Nations 4.30

American Craft Museum

In contrast with the historically oriented Museum of American Folk Art (see page 6.18), the American Craft Museum focuses on contemporary craft objects. Temporary exhibitions emphasise the aesthetic value of functional objects, such as quilts, furniture, clothing, jewellery, and table-ware. One recent exhibition, 'Brooching it Diplomatically', in response to Madeleine Albright's habit of voicing her political views through her choice of jewellery, invited artists to design their own brooches for the Secretary of State.

Established in 1956, the American Craft Museum moved in 1986 to a space more like that of the surrounding up-market boutiques than that of a museum. Indeed, pride of place is given to the institution's colossal shop, while some of the galleries are crowded and poorly lit. The museum sponsors educational activities, workshops, guided tours, and symposia.

ADDRESS 40 West 53rd Street (between Fifth and Sixth Avenues), New York, NY 10019; (212) 956 3535
OPEN Tuesday to Sunday, 10.00–18.00; Thursday, 10.00–20.00
ADMISSION $5; students and seniors $2.50
DISABILITY ACCESS full
SUBWAY E, F to Fifth Avenue and 53rd Street; 1, 9 to 50th Street; B, D, F, Q to 47th–50th Streets

Americas Society

Founded in 1965, and housed in a handsome McKim, Mead & White mansion on Park Avenue, the Americas Society has a unique mission: it informs inhabitants of the USA about the political, economic, and cultural life of Latin America, the Caribbean, and Canada. Whatever cold-war imperatives may have influenced the founding of the Society, thinking about the Americas as a group is a compelling and much neglected intellectual project, and serves to correct American – whoops, I mean US – exceptionalism.

   The Americas Society hosts three exhibitions a year in a single, well articulated gallery space of moderate size. Given the breadth of its project, the Society does a good job of maintaining a capacious, yet sufficiently specific focus in each of these exhibitions. Broad geographic surveys are counterbalanced by chronological specificity, and vice versa. Exhibitions scheduled for the first few years of the new century, for example, include '2000 Years of Peruvian Silver', and 'Abstract Art from the Río de la Plata, 1933–1953'.

   Around these shows, the society organises comprehensive programmes of bilingual lectures and symposia. The Western Hemisphere division arranges panel discussions on political, economic, and social issues, while Cultural Affairs offers concerts, film screenings, literary readings and writers' workshops.

ADDRESS 680 Park Avenue, New York, NY 10021; (212) 249 8950
OPEN Tuesday to Sunday, 11.00–18.00
ADMISSION $3.00; students and seniors $2.00
DISABILITY ACCESS limited (telephone in advance of visit)
SUBWAY 6 to 68th Street

Intrepid Sea Air Space Museum

If you're not easily won over by the sinister glamour of weaponry, or turned on by American military history, you may be unimpressed by this aircraft carrier-cum-museum. Nonetheless, the Intrepid as sheer mass is undeniably a sight to behold. The aircraft carrier is 900 feet long and stocked with a bevy of aircraft that you can examine up close on deck, and is permanently docked at Pier 86 on the Hudson River. There are a variety of exhibits housed inside the ship, and you can tour the missile submarine and destroyer parked close by. The destroyer, Edson, is perhaps the least compelling of the exhibits, as there is relatively little to see: visitors merely clamber around the deck and peer at control panels. Located right next to it, the Growler works better as a tourist attraction, as it offers visitors the rare opportunity to see the inside of a submarine. (The museum claims that it is the only intact guided missile submarine in the world that is open to the public.) If you plan to see it all, the Intrepid museum is literally a lot of ground to cover: this, together with a typical wait of an hour for the submarine tour, accounts for the fact that the museum recommends a one-to-four hour time allotment for your visit.

The museum was originally the brainchild of Zachary Fisher, a philanthropist and supporter of the armed forces, who established the Intrepid Museum Foundation in 1978 in order to prevent the aircraft carrier from being turned into scrap. The 'Sea-Air-Space' version of the museum opened four years later, with the historic Intrepid as its centrepiece.

Launched in 1943, the Intrepid participated in World War II and also served as a recovery vessel for NASA, picking up the Mercury and Gemini capsules (hence the 'space' component of the museum). The exhibits inside are thus devoted to these events and to military history more generally. Some of these, such as 'Air War over Europe, 1939–1945' and

4.8

'George Bush: His World War II Years', are distinctly uninspired, but the wide range of aircraft on display (some dating back to as early as 1917) is more stimulating. Recently, the museum has been making a concerted effort to update its image by adding interactive elements: the Desert Storm Strike Simulator and A-6 Cockpit Challenge, both high-tech rides which simulate flight, have been well received, and even less tech-y hands-on displays, such as one on the history of flight with a pedal-operated human-powered plane, seem to be providing the museum with some new, and necessary, energy.

ADDRESS Pier 86, West 46th Street and Twelfth Avenue, New York, NY 10036; (212) 245-0072; www.intrepid-museum.com
OPEN Wednesday to Sunday, 10.00–17.00 (winter) and Monday to Friday, 10.00–17.00 (summer)
ADMISSION $10 (telephone for numerous discount offerings)
DISABILITY ACCESS limited
SUBWAY any line to 42nd Street; then crosstown bus M42

midtown

Japan Society

Located a few doors down from the United Nations, the Japan Society seeks to promote understanding between the USA and Japan. The institution was founded in 1907 by prominent Japanese and American businessmen of New York. After closing during WWII, the Japan Society resumed its activities under the leadership of John D Rockefeller III. The Society's current home, completed in 1971 by the architect Junzo Yoshimura, was the first building of contemporary Japanese design in New York. Especially after its remodelling in 1997, the building's interior is spectacular. A central atrium runs through four floors and contains several indoor gardens, one of which is connected to the lower-level pool by a waterfall. The galleries and administrative space wind around the atrium, and the rather dark and calm exhibition space provides a dramatic contrast to the central column of sunlight and vegetation.

Permanent and temporary exhibitions, often mounted in collaboration with impressive private and public collections, include screens, scrolls, ceramics, prints, calligraphy, and tea equipment. While the exhibitions tend to focus on high art of historical provenance, the Society hosts an astonishing array of programmes, including theatre, music and films from Kurosawa to Akira. Lectures and panels address topics as far apart as Pokémon and the sacred arts, with speakers ranging from contemporary artist Mariko Mori to Japan's first female astronaut.

ADDRESS 333 East 47th Street, New York, NY 10017; (212) 832 1155; www.jpnsoc.org
OPEN Tuesday to Sunday, 11.00–18.00
ADMISSION (suggested) $5
DISABILITY ACCESS full
SUBWAY 6 to 51st Street; E, F to 53rd Street

The Morgan Library

The illuminated manuscripts, rare editions, and graphic artworks here make fascinating objects in themselves. But perhaps even more compelling is the infrastructure that gives form to the collection. Although, since Morgan's death in 1913, the library has opened its doors to the public and the collection has quadrupled, acquisitions have quite strictly followed the imperatives that Morgan set when he first established his private library. Consequently, whether such rigorous adherence to Morgan's original plan is a salutary policy or not, the Morgan Library tells us as much about American attitudes to high culture at the turn of the century as it does about early modern print and manuscript culture.

The prominent financier Morgan amassed an impressive collection of books toward the end of the nineteenth century – a period of astonishingly rapid economic growth in the USA, and particularly in New York. In 1906, the holdings outgrew the home, and Morgan hired the architectural firm of McKim, Mead & White to design a Renaissance-style palazzo. The design of the building reflects the Gilded Age vogue for classical architecture, as does the content of the library's collection, which focuses on the heritage of the Italian Renaissance. Formally and thematically, the interior expresses the humanist conviction in the unity of the arts: architecture, the plastic arts, and text are harmoniously blended. The central rotunda combines Doric pilasters, freestanding marble columns, and an arched portico with sculpture and allegorical ceiling paintings. A lunette above the building's entrance bears the emblem of the Italian Renaissance printer Aldus borne aloft by cherubs.

The West Room remains a sumptuous personal monument to Morgan. It was here that he began to assemble a collection of books on the model of the gentleman's library, as opposed to the scholarly collection. Adorned with Renaissance paintings and topped by an antique wooden ceiling

purchased in Florence and reconstructed on site, this private library was oriented to social display. The East Room reflects the extent to which nineteenth-century American curatorial imperatives were divided between the goal of establishing a distinctly American cultural identity – one that could vie with Europe's – and aping Europe's cultural refinement. In the ornamental gold leaf, the designers strove to reproduce the tonal qualities of an old Florentine frame. Muted, restrained colours were chosen in order to give the room a patina that would dissemble its newness.

The Morgan continues to grow in both collections (especially prints and drawings) and display space. In 1991, the museum opened a pleasant glass-enclosed conservatory and café, full of ivy and sunlight, thus linking the original Morgan house with the Library Annex.

ADDRESS 29 East 36th Street, New York, NY 10016; (212) 685 0610; www.morganlibrary.org
OPEN Tuesday to Thursday, 10.30–17.00; Friday, 10.30–20.00; Saturday, 10.30–18.00; Sunday, 12.00–18.00
ADMISSION $7; students and seniors $5; free to children under 12 with an adult
DISABILITY ACCESS slightly limited (wheelchairs available)
SUBWAY 6 to 33rd Street; 4, 5, 6, 7 to Grand Central; B, D, F, Q to 42nd Street

midtown

The Museum of Modern Art (MoMA)

Indisputably one of the most influential museums in the world, MOMA established itself as a cultural touchstone at its inception in 1929, when it became the first museum to devote its collection exclusively to modern art. A forerunner in admitting architecture, design, photography and film into twentieth-century definitions of art, MOMA still has leading holdings in each of these genres. Its film library, for instance, has the foremost international collection in the USA, and holds all the surviving original negatives of the Biograph and Edison companies, as well as the world's most comprehensive collection of D W Griffith films. The Painting and Sculpture Department is equally prominent: considered the largest collection of modern art in the world, it contains more than 3200 works dating from the 1880s to the present. If it's not yet obvious what a truly comprehensive collection of twentieth-century art would look like, the MOMA's – with its iconic pieces like Van Gogh's *Starry Night* and Warhol's *Marilyn* – is assuredly a representative one.

MOMA's website may perform a similarly definitional function for the twenty-first century. Operating as a museum in its own right, the site makes works from all current exhibitions available for users to view and engage with, thanks to a number of extremely well designed interactive features. Some innovative art projects mounted there are designed specifically for on-line use and viewing. There is also a searchable database with an index of artists that allows you to see internet versions of major special exhibitions conducted by MOMA in the past. The site's 'Dadabase' can be searched for library, archival and study centre information, and a special site for children and their parents takes visitors on an 'art safari'.

The museum's extra-curricular activities include one of the best retrospective film programmes in the country, weekly jazz and classical music concerts at its café, and an extensive series of lectures and talks. Its attrac-

The Museum of Modern Art (MoMA)

4.18

tive sculpture garden (designed by Philip Johnson and added on to the museum in 1953) can serve as an oasis in which to rest between galleries – when it's not overcrowded with others responding to the same impulse. MOMA has ambitious plans for the renovation and extension of its current space, set to take place in the first few years of the new century. Designed by Yoshio Taniguchi, the new version of the museum will include an education and research complex, an additional theatre, and a doubling of its existing gallery space.

ADDRESS 11 West 53rd Street (between Fifth and Sixth Avenues), New York, NY 10019; (212) 708 9400; www.moma.org
OPEN Monday, Tuesday, Thursday, Saturday, Sunday, 10.30–17.45, Friday, 10.30–21.00
ADMISSION $10; students and seniors $6.50; children under 16 free; Friday 16.30–20.15, pay what you wish
DISABILITY ACCESS full (telephone or visit website for more information about special services)
SUBWAY E, F to Fifth Avenue/53rd Street

midtown

Museum of TV & Radio

Named after the museum's founder, the William S Paley building was designed by Philip Johnson and its bold yet functional neo-Gothic design complements the populist sensibility of the collection within. Based on the idea that television and radio productions, regardless of their artistic value, are important embodiments of collective memory and of cultural-historical meaning, the museum was set up in 1975 to archive these forms and make them broadly available to the public.

Surprisingly, considering that this is a country devoted to the hoarding of culture, no major archive of TV and radio existed in the USA before the museum came into being. As a result, many historic TV moments, such as the first address from the White House and the first Super Bowl, have no known copies in existence. In order to forestall future losses such as these, the Museum not only preserves programmes but also transfers them to digital videotape to avoid deterioration during duplication. More than 100,000 television and radio programmes from the last 75 years are housed in its archives, including news shows, documentaries, comedies, children's shows and commercial advertising. Upon placing a request, visitors can watch or listen to shows of their choice at individual radio or TV consoles.

If you don't have time to request and watch a show, you can wander through the museum's exhibits of highlights from its collection. Screenings of popular TV moments – such as Robin Williams' stand-up comedy – display cases of costumes from *Star Trek*, and listening consoles that showcase legendary radio shows such as *The Shadow* are a sample of past offerings. For the most entertaining experience, though, plan to request one or more shows and spend an afternoon wallowing in nostalgia not dependent on the programming tastes of Nick at Nite. The museum also hosts seminars, screenings and educational programmes designed to

THE MUSEUM OF TELEVISION & RADIO

foster critical thinking about the media, such as a recent seminar on 'Television and Terrorism'. It has a duplicate collection in Los Angeles, in a building fittingly located in Beverly Hills and designed by another star architect, Richard Meier.

ADDRESS 25 West 52 Street (between Fifth and Sixth Avenues), New York, NY 10019; (212) 621 6800; www.mtr.org
OPEN Tuesday to Sunday, 12.00–18.00; Thursday, 12.00–20.00; Friday, 12.00–21.00
ADMISSION (suggested) $6; students $4; children under 13, $3
DISABILITY ACCESS full (assisted listening devices also available)
SUBWAY E or F to Fifth Avenue

Newseum/NY

The original Newseum debuted in 1997 in Arlington, VA. An interactive museum set up to teach visitors about news production, news coverage and the history of news journalism, it is run by the non-partisan organisation, Freedom Forum: a group designed to promote freedom and fairness of the press. Newseum/NY is a smaller, less interactive organisation whose exhibitions focus on photojournalism. It also organises lectures, films and other public-outreach activities designed to widen debates about the role of the press and First Amendment issues.

Situated in the lobby of the massive IBM building, the museum's exhibition space is its least attractive quality: its bland amalgam of contemporary corporate design clichés never allows you to forget that you're in an office lobby. To some degree, the surroundings befit the museum's straightforward-bordering-on-simple-minded approach to its subject-matter. The text accompanying photos tends to rely too much on the glibness of sound-bites, and the exhibits, though topical and usually interesting in subject-matter, beg to be presented in a more creative and thought-provoking manner. Recent and up-coming exhibitions range from 'Gun Nation', photographs depicting America's fascination with guns, to 'Full Moon', which covers 30 years of lunar photo-journalism. Programmes run by the museum include an author series, media roundtables, and international programmes that examine worldwide media issues.

ADDRESS 580 Madison Avenue (between 56th and 57th Streets), New York, NY 10022; (212) 317 7503; www.newseum.org
OPEN Monday to Saturday, 10.00–17.30
ADMISSION free
DISABILITY ACCESS full
SUBWAY N, R to Fifth Avenue

The New York Public Library

The New York Public Library was conceived when New York had no public library as such: it incorporated two of the city's most outstanding quasi-public libraries, the collections of John Jacob Astor and James Lenox. The opulent Beaux-Arts building – with its imposing sculptures of lions, elegant façade, grand marble staircases, and elaborately decorated ceilings – was designed by the then relatively unknown architectural firm of Carrère and Hastings, and was completed in 1911 at a final cost of 29 million dollars.

One of the world's greatest libraries, the New York Public must also be counted as one of the city's most significant museums. In the four galleries of the Humanities and Social Sciences Library at 42nd Street, the subjects of temporary exhibitions range from Truman Capote to King Arthur. Among the Library's collection, which numbers more than 50 million items, many of the textual holdings are also highly significant as objects in themselves, such as Jefferson's handwritten copy of the Declaration of Independence, and a Gutenberg Bible which was the first in the New World. Moreover, the collection of artefacts ranges from objects of world-historical significance to everyday ephemera – indeed, from cuneiform tablets to restaurant menus.

A broad variety of collections rival those of the city's more specialised museums. The collection of photographs is especially strong in stereoscopic views. The library holds more maps than any other public library in the USA, and a formidable array of films, prints, CD-ROMS and government documents. While visiting the main branch, drop in on the newly-renovated Bill Blass reading room. Orient your visit by picking up a few of the many flyers available at the entrances.

Among The New York Public Library's many branches, The Schomburg Center for Research in Black Culture is especially impressive.

midtown

The New York Public Library

Named after a librarian and curator who was also an active figure in the Harlem renaissance and an early historian of black culture, the Schomburg possesses more than five million books and artefacts, including an impressive number of rare first editions of slave narratives and African-American poetry. It is perhaps the world's foremost research library for African-American culture and literature. Temporary exhibitions display African and African-American art, religious and cultural artefacts, and photographs of black leaders in music, literature, and politics. The Schomburg also hosts plays, concerts, readings and films.

Humanities and Social Sciences Library:
ADDRESS Fifth Avenue and 42nd Street, New York, NY 10018; (212) 869 8089; www.nypl.org
OPEN Monday to Friday 10.00–19.00; Saturday, 10.00–18.00; Sunday, 12.00–17.00
ADMISSION free
DISABILITY ACCESS full
SUBWAY 1, 2, 3, 9 to 42nd Street/Times Square; B, D, F, Q to 42nd Street

Schomburg Center:
ADDRESS 515 Malcolm X Boulevard, New York, NY 10037; (212) 491 2200; www.nypl.org/research/sc/sc.html
OPEN Monday to Saturday, 10.00–18.00; Sunday 13.00–17.00
ADMISSION free
DISABILITY ACCESS full
SUBWAY 2, 3 to 135th Street

midtown

United Nations

Though the United Nations' exterior appears dated, the public tour does much to promote its democratic agenda and ongoing achievements. Founded after WWII to foster peace, social progress and human rights, the UN currently has 185 member states. Most of its decisions are made from its headquarters in New York, a complex which functions as 'international territory' and feels like it. Once past the metal detectors at the entry, America drops away and the babel of tourists, diplomats, and UN officials from all over the world dominates.

The UN has agglomerated a medley of peace symbols expressed through art, including sculptures, paintings, tapestries and other artefacts. Remnants of coins, cans and bowls from Hiroshima and Nagasaki are on display, as is the original charter of the UN, signed in 1945. Visitors can use a meditation room devoted to world peace or peruse a topical art exhibition in the lobby. The tour provides information about the functions of the UN, and takes in the Economic and Social Council Chambers, the General Assembly Hall, and the Security Council Chambers. Tourguides even provide diverting trivia: the fact that scuba divers are stationed in the East River during General Assembly meetings in anticipation of emergencies was a revelation to me. Outside the building are a number of highly symbolic sculptures – including a Japanese peace bell and a Russian statue, 'Let us beat swords into ploughshares'.

ADDRESS First Avenue at East 46th Street New York, NY 10017; (212) 963 7713; www.un.org
OPEN Monday to Sunday, 9.15–17.45; closed weekends January/February
ADMISSION $7.50; seniors, $5.50; students $4.50; children $3.50
DISABILITY ACCESS full (wheelchairs available for guided tours)
SUBWAY 4, 5, 6, 7 to 42nd Street/Grand Central; then M42 to First Avenue

upper east side

The Mount Vernon Hotel Museum and Garden 5.2
Asia Society 5.6
Cooper-Hewitt, National Design Museum 5.8
El Museo del Barrio 5.12
The Frick Collection 5.16
Solomon R Guggenheim Museum 5.20
International Center of Photography 5.24
The Jewish Museum 5.26
Metropolitan Museum of Art 5.30
Museum of the City of New York 5.34
National Academy of Design 5.38
Whitney Museum of American Art 5.40

The Mount Vernon Hotel Museum and Garden

The house was first conceived in 1795 as part of an ambitious 23-acre country estate planned by Abigail Adams Smith (daughter of John Adams) and her husband, Colonel William Stephens Smith. Faced with financial difficulties, the couple sold the estate to a prosperous New York merchant only a year later, and 'Smith's Folly' was completed according to a much reduced version of their plans. In 1826, its H-shaped carriage house was converted into the Mount Vernon Hotel, one of the many in this area that served as elegant country resorts for weary city residents. Four miles north of the city, the Mount Vernon made a refreshing stop during an evening carriage ride and afforded a pleasant view over the east river. Consequently, the museum tells us less about the Smiths than it does about resort life in the early nineteenth century. Indeed, the Smiths' planning of the estate and their subsequent loss of it is merely the beginning of a series of episodes through which the house reflects the shifting forms of American gentility.

After the area declined during the nineteenth century, the house was sold to what is now Con Edison. There is some irony in the fact that the preservation of the house owes much to the placement around it of three large ugly storage tanks, which discouraged prospective buyers once Con Edison no longer used the space, and thus saved it from being purchased and remodelled.

The museum took its present form after it was purchased in 1924 by something called The Colonial Dames of America, and it was opened in 1939 to coincide with the New York World's Fair. These, um, dames have done a fine job of restoring the house, even if the museum lacks the antiquarian rigour of institutions like the Morris-Jumel Mansion. What remains of the hotel's original furnishings has been complemented by

somewhat approximate period pieces. The blend of parochial and elegant qualities in the salon is particularly charming. A small but very pleasant eighteenth-century-style garden runs along the back of the house.

The organisation which runs the museum also runs informative tours as well as a modest series of lectures and concerts.

ADDRESS 421 East 61st Street (between First and York Avenues), New York, NY 10021; (212) 838 6878
OPEN Tuesday to Sunday, 11.00–16.00 (Tuesday to 21.00 June and July; closed in August)
ADMISSION $4; $3 students and seniors; free for children under 12
DISABILITY ACCESS by appointment only (special tour available for visually impaired)
SUBWAY R, N, 4, 5, 6 to 59th Street

The Mount Vernon Hotel Museum and Garden

Asia Society

The Asia Society was founded in 1956 with the mission of promoting understanding between Asian nations, and building American awareness of the cultures of Asia and the Pacific Islands. The latter goal is reflected in the materials of the building (designed in 1981 by Edward Larrabee Barnes), a mixture of red sandstone from Rajasthan, India, and polished red granite from Oklahoma.

The aim of developing a capacious perspective on Asia – one not focused on Japan and China to the detriment of the rest of the continent – provides the institution with a rather formidable challenge. It is perhaps out of a sense of the daunting nature of this comprehensive vision that the curators have limited the permanent gallery to a smallish space that can show only a fraction of the extensive collections at any given time.

Upstairs from this assortment of Korean ceramics, Indian miniatures, Japanese Buddhist paintings, Indonesian textiles, and Thai sculptures is a gallery for more focused temporary exhibitions. The quality of these exhibitions is such that I no longer worry about whether the topic interests me – I just go. The Asia Society also hosts a vibrant series of performances, films, and lectures.

Until fall 2001 the museum is located at 502 Park Avenue (at 59th Street).

ADDRESS 725 Park Avenue (at 70th Street), New York, NY 10021; (212) 288 6400; www.asiasociety.org
OPEN Tuesday to Saturday, 11.00–18.00; Thursday until 20.00 (free 18.00–20.00)
ADMISSION $4; students and seniors $2
DISABILITY ACCESS full
SUBWAY 6 to 68th Street

Cooper-Hewitt, National Design Museum

The Cooper-Hewitt was originally conceived by Peter Cooper, but also bears the name of his granddaughters, Eleanor and Sarah Hewitt, who formally opened the museum in 1897. Cooper, who founded Cooper Union in downtown Manhattan in 1859 to provide workers with higher education in art and technology, had envisaged the museum as a school of instruction for professional designers and workers, but the Hewitts eventually established it as an important collection as well. Inspired by the Musée des Arts Décoratifs in Paris, they collected a wide range of materials, including patterns, textiles, scrapbooks, paintings, sketches and drawings: a significant proportion of the fine arts collection was filled out by donations from the estates of Winslow Homer and Frederic E Church. The museum became part of the Smithsonian in 1967 and moved to its current residence in 1976 – an extravagant 64-room Fifth Avenue mansion complete with conservatory and terraced garden, that was once home to Andrew Carnegie.

Despite the posh traditional demeanour of its exterior, the museum's exhibitions can be decidedly hip. Focusing particularly on the interaction of aesthetics and utility in the design of everyday objects, its recent exhibitions have broadened definitions of the subject to explore everything from the vernacular urban landscape of Latino Los Angeles to the 'Architecture of Reassurance' at Disneyland. An important 1998 exhibition, 'Unlimited by Design', investigated the radical potential of 'universal design' – the idea that everyday objects should reduce physical barriers between people of different ages and abilities. The permanent collection serves as a vital resource for students, scholars, designers and collectors, and consists of four departments: Applied Arts and Industrial Design, Drawings and Prints, Textiles, and Wallcoverings. Though specialists will

Cooper-Hewitt, National Design Museum

be particularly interested in these holdings, they are open to everyone (by appointment) and contain a truly staggering range of objects. The wall-coverings collection is especially fascinating, ranging from William Morris-inspired prints to nineteenth-century French floral patterns to Dutch gilded leather designs.

Visitors can also access the well-stocked library and the Archives. Offering a range of information on individual designers and design firms, the Archives include recently added African-American and Latino/Hispanic sections. Though the staid design of the garden may strike you as uninspired after your perusal of the museum's holdings, it's worth visiting just for the thrill of standing on a lawn on Fifth Avenue – but telephone ahead to find out if it's open.

ADDRESS 2 East 91st (at Fifth Avenue), New York, NY 10128; (212) 849 8387; www.si.edu/ndm/
OPEN Tuesday, 10.00–21.00; Wednesday to Saturday, 10.00–17.00; Sunday, 12.00–17.00
ADMISSION $8; seniors and students $5; members and children under 12 free; Tuesday 17.00–21.00 free
DISABILITY ACCESS full (for information about sign-language tours, call (212) 860 6899; TDD (212) 860 6865)
SUBWAY 4, 5, 6 to 86th Street

El Museo del Barrio

Along with many other artistic projects of the period, El Museo del Barrio was inspired by the national civil rights movement of the 1960s. Established in 1969 by a group of Puerto Rican artists, educators and activists from East Harlem's *el barrio* community, the museum sees itself as both a neighbourhood cultural centre and an artistic forum dedicated to 'preserving and projecting the cultural heritage of Puerto Ricans and all Latin Americans in the United States'. Its permanent collection holds a significant array of Caribbean and Latin American art objects and artefacts (approximately 8000 objects in total), including photographs, drawings, sculptures, and videos, while temporary exhibitions have included off-site and site-specific installations, such as Martha Chilindron's amazing *Cinema Kinesis*, a life-size motorised pop-up movie theatre. The pieces range from the traditional – such as those shown in its 1997 Taíno exhibition of pre-Columbian art and culture from the Caribbean – to the contemporary, as exemplified by its recent show of graphic work by Brooklyn-born artist-activist Juan Sánchez. By shifting its focus from the old to the new and back again, the museum's exhibitions highlight the disparate ways in which Latin American identity can be conceived. From one show to the next, organisational guidelines as various as religious, national, aesthetic and geographical affinities might be used.

Once housed in a schoolroom, the museum is now located in the commodious neo-classical Heckscher Building on Fifth Avenue. Still part of *el barrio* but also positioned alongside the art establishment on Museum Mile, El Museo is advantageously situated to address diverse audiences. By hosting a number of community events and educational initiatives, including studio walks and mural walks in the surrounding neighbourhood, the museum ensures that art in the community and that

El Museo del Barrio

located in the museum are explicitly co-extensive. Family and community outreach programmes, often organised around cultural festivals such as the Day of the Dead, involve visitors in art projects based on current exhibitions. While its allegiance to the neighbourhood remains a priority, the museum's reach has begun to extend far beyond the community as well – visitor numbers have quintupled over the last five years. To commemorate the millennium, El Museo will open a renovated version of the Heckscher Theater – a spacious 1920s theatre with original murals – as well as a Latin American-themed restaurant and an expanded version of its already excellent gift shop.

ADDRESS 1230 Fifth Avenue (at 104th Street), New York, NY 10029; (212) 831 7272; www.elmuseo.org
OPEN Wednesday to Sunday, 11.00–17.00
ADMISSION $4 (suggested); students and seniors $2; children under 12 free
DISABILITY ACCESS full
SUBWAY 6 to 103rd Street

The Frick Collection

This stunning neo-classical mansion, one of the most lavish settings for the public exhibition of art in the USA, was originally designed by Thomas Hastings as home to steel magnate Henry Clay Frick. (The commission for Frick's mansion followed on the renown won by the Carrère and Hastings firm in gaining the contract for the New York Public Library.) The greater part of this extensive collection was amassed by Frick himself before his death in 1919: it opened to the public in 1935. The museum's moderate size and its focus on European masters of the fourteenth through nineteenth centuries make it a good antidote to New York's more comprehensive museums. The gorgeous interior courtyard and fountain, the formal gardens, the ornate wood panelling of each room – everything in the Frick bespeaks sumptuousness.

Unfortunately, the museum tells us about Frick himself a little too often. I had a particularly simulacral experience in the atrium, when, attempting to locate the source of conspicuously live-sounding organ music, I was informed that it was a recording of concerts played on the Aeolian pipe organ that Frick had installed in the mansion. The audio-phone tour includes commentary not only on the history of the collections, but also on the history of the house and Frick's life. Choices that now seem eccentric continue to mark the collection: he collected no American artists except for Whistler (and, perhaps for its subject more than for the painter, Gilbert Stuart's famous portrait of George Washington). Moreover, with two exceptions, he prudishly excluded nudes – from a formidable collection of Renaissance and neo-classical art!

Whatever the Frick's drawbacks, they are minor in comparison to the splendour of the collection, which was amassed under the guidance of art dealer Joseph Duveen and the noted art historian Roger Fry. The collection is particularly strong in Rembrandt, Hals, Vermeer, Goya, and

The Frick Collection

Frick's favourite, Van Dyck. Don't miss Bellini's *Saint Francis in Ecstasy*, or the delicious Fragonard Room. Four of the panels were commissioned for Madame du Barry, who refused them. The collections of Renaissance bronzes and eighteenth-century French sculpture are among the world's finest.

The Frick is now attempting to combat its clubby, inaccessible image. Though the prohibition of children under ten is not likely to be lifted, the entranceway has been revamped with the aim of making the museum feel more accessible. Also, the Frick runs a website with an impressive three-dimensional tour.

ADDRESS 1 East 70th Street (at Fifth Avenue) New York, NY 10021; (212) 288 0700; www.frick.org
OPEN Tuesday to Saturday, 10.00–18.00; Sunday, 13.00–18.00
ADMISSION $7, $5 students and seniors (children under ten not admitted; children under 16 must be accompanied by an adult)
DISABILITY ACCESS full (wheelchairs available)
SUBWAY: 6 to 68th Street

Solomon R Guggenheim Museum

'Here is the ideal I propose for the architecture of the machine age, for how an ideal American architecture should develop in the image of trees.' Thus did Frank Lloyd Wright describe the now iconic building he designed for the Guggenheim museum. Though visionary in artistic outlook from its inception, the museum's reputation as a shrine to modernist art and ideals was sealed once it took up residence in the building in 1959 (also the year that Wright died). Debates about the Guggenheim often centre around whether its brilliant spiral architecture eclipses rather than complements the art within. The most recently built structure in the city to have been designated a New York landmark, the Guggenheim, influenced by Wright's study of ancient Mesopotamian ziggurats, stands in deliberate contrast to the sober linearity of the buildings around it. Ingeniously designed so as to allow light into each level of the spiral, the architecture acts out the modernist principles of the art within by underscoring the subjectivity of perception: the art offers different perspectives depending where you are on the spiral. The 1992 addition to the building – a ten-storey tower with spacious galleries – now allows the museum to accommodate larger installations. The extension also includes a sculpture terrace that connects the old and new sections as well as the interior and exterior spaces of the building, thereby creating a dynamic space that does justice to Wright's original organic vision.

Originally named the Museum of Non-Objective Painting, the collection was first established by Solomon R Guggenheim and his artist-advisor friend Hilla Rebay in 1939 as a home for avant-garde art. As its name suggested, the collection was devoted largely to modern European painters such as Kandinsky, Chagall, Léger, and Delaunay. By the early 1940s, the museum's collection included pioneering work by early abstract expressionists as well, including Mark Rothko, Jackson Pollock

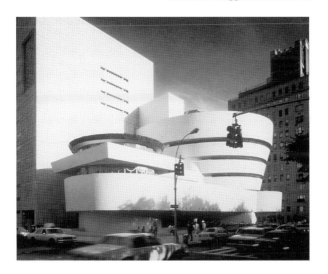

and Robert Motherwell. Since then, the museum has remained strongly identified with the modern art that makes up the core of its collection, even though it houses contemporary art as well.

While the Guggenheim has been labelled a 'cathedral of art', it has also been called an art 'super-garage' because of the way the spiral propels visitors past the exhibits. Both the high modernist conception of Wright's building and the more populist 'garage' idea are particularly relevant now that the museum has begun to mount more crowd-pleasing shows, such as its 1998 'Art of the Motorcycle'. Whether its recent courtship of larger audiences with less abstract exhibits is a cynical financial move or a new form of avant-gardism is still the subject of controversy.

As part of its pioneering self-image, the museum prides itself on being the first international museum; it is affiliated with the Peggy Guggenheim museum in Venice, the Deutsche Guggenheim Berlin, and the much publicised new Guggenheim museum in Bilbao, designed by Frank O Gehry as a tribute to Wright. Its downtown branch in Soho, however, once a dynamic component of the museum's New York presence, has recently given way to a Prada store. Though one lone floor of the museum still houses a semi-permanent exhibition of Andy Warhol's The Last Supper, its future is uncertain.

ADDRESS 1071 Fifth Avenue (at 89th Street), New York, NY 10128; (212) 423 3500; www.guggenheim.org/solomon/
OPEN Sunday to Wednesday, 9.00–18.00; Friday, Saturday, 9.00–20.00
ADMISSION $12; students and seniors $7; children under 12 free
DISABILITY ACCESS full (telephone for details)
SUBWAY 4, 5, 6 to 86th Street

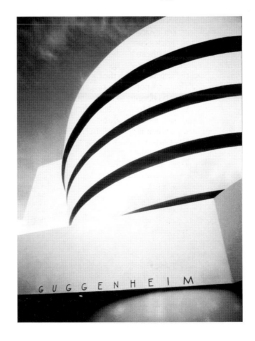

upper east side

International Center of Photography

Split between locations on Museum Mile and in midtown, the ICP grew out of the International Fund for Concerned Photography, founded in 1966 by Cornell Capa. While the midtown location houses darkroom facilities, offers extensive educational programmes, and mounts exhibitions of student photographs, the uptown space is devoted exclusively to the display of major photographs. Temporary exhibitions have featured work ranging from Muybridge to the Starn twins, while the permanent collection focuses on early twentieth-century work, emphasising photojournalism and documentary photography. Archival holdings include substantial collections of works by Berenice Abbott, Henri Cartier-Bresson, Robert and Cornell Capa, Weegee, and Diane Arbus.

Though the ICP concentrates on photography, the Center takes seriously the intersection of photography with print, electronic, and digital media. The library (at the uptown location – telephone for opening hours) holds over 8000 volumes, and 10,000 back issues of art magazines. Photographs and artist biographies are accessible online. Both locations run screening rooms for exhibition-related videos and films.

OPEN Tuesday to Thursday, 10.00–17.00; Friday, 10.00–20.00; Saturday, Sunday, 10.00–18.00
ADMISSION $6; students and seniors $4; children under 12 $1
Museum Mile: address 1130 Fifth Avenue (at 94th Street), New York, NY 10128; (212) 860 1777; www.icp.org
DISABILITY ACCESS limited (telephone in advance)
SUBWAY 4, 5, 6 to 96th Street
Midtown: address 1133 Avenue of the Americas (Sixth Avenue at 43rd Street), New York, NY 10036; (212) 768 4682
DISABILITY ACCESS full
SUBWAY B, D, F, Q to 42nd Street/Times Square; 1, 2, 3, 9, N, R, 7 to 42nd Street

The Jewish Museum

The challenge that this museum faces is how to make intelligible 4000 years of Jewish history – and the various meanings of such a term across time, space, and different levels of cultural experience. The museum's response is not to downplay the inherent difficulties in such a task, nor to resort to a narrow definition of what constitutes Jewish identity, but to extend the challenge to the visitor through its attention to the variety, permeability, and adaptability of Jewish culture. Consequently, exhibits not only address ritual, religious law, and community-building, but also consider what's Jewish about topics as diverse as television and psychoanalysis.

Modern art, text, ceremonial artefacts, ritual and quotidian dress, and documentary photographs combine in a series of thoughtful displays that are arranged in a roughly chronological sequence. A room devoted to the Sabbath, for example, includes antique scriptures, paintings by Max Weber, and even piped-in music. The Museum's stewardship maintains the tension between preserving tradition and offering a critique of it, often juxtaposing ritual art objects with the work of contemporary artists such as Sophie Calle or Adrian Piper. Signage adroitly addresses issues specific to documenting a diasporic culture, such as the geographical provenance of artefacts that circulate from Palestine to Georgia, or between Venice and Central Asia.

The history of the Jewish Museum goes back to 1904, when private donations of artefacts and artworks were assembled under the auspices of the Jewish Theological Seminary of America. During the next half-century, that crucial time for Jewish diasporic consciousness, the collections continued to grow, and, in 1947, the museum opened in its present home, a French Gothic-style mansion on Fifth Avenue. After expansions in 1963 and 1993, the ornate limestone façade of the original residence

The Jewish Museum

upper east side

The Jewish Museum

was extended, and there is now a pleasant kosher café with stained-glass windows. The museum's public programmes include films, panel discussions, and a variety of concerts ranging from jazz to Middle-Eastern music.

ADDRESS 1109 Fifth Avenue, New York, NY 10128; (212) 423 3224; www.thejewishmuseum.org
OPEN Sunday, Monday, Wednesday, Thursday, 11.00–17.45; Tuesday, 11.00–20.00
ADMISSION $8; students and seniors $5.50; free Tuesday 17.00–20.00; children under 12 free
DISABILITY ACCESS full
SUBWAY 4, 5, 6 to 86th Street

Metropolitan Museum of Art

The Metropolitan was founded in 1870 by a group of American financiers and artists, and it moved to the sparsely inhabited area around Central Park ten years later. The building has undergone a good deal of refurbishment and expansion since Edith Wharton's Newland Archer and Madame Olenska met in 'the queer wilderness of cast-iron and encaustic tiles known as the Metropolitan Museum'. Additions now completely surround the original Gothic Revival building. The central section was designed by Richard Morris Hunt in 1902, the side wings by McKim, Mead & White in 1906, and gallery space has more than doubled since the late 1970s.

According to the encyclopedic imperatives that have shaped the Met's collections, the museum should be virtually indescribable; and it is. Out of more than three million works of art in the permanent collection, several hundred thousand are on view at any given time. The museum also hosts more than 30 special exhibitions each year, and contains eight textual and photographic libraries. Many of the Met's departments are extensive enough to constitute a museum in themselves, and are best visited as such.

First-time visitors will not want to miss the exhibitions of Renaissance European and near eastern art. The latter department was formed as recently as 1956: the works in the collection range over 70 centuries. Also, the American Wing constitutes one of the most comprehensive collections of American painting and sculpture in the world (though its endpoint is the early twentieth century). Its collection in the decorative arts includes a Frank Lloyd Wright living room and a stair hall by the firm of McKim, Mead & White. For those who have already visited the museum several times, recent additions include the Antonio Ratti Textile Center, the Cyprus galleries, and galleries devoted to the

art of South and Southeast Asia.

The museum offers a constant flow of programmes (rarely fewer than five on a given day), consisting of lectures, gallery talks and films. The Met's musical concerts – often under-publicised and under-appreciated in New York – are first-rate. Walking tours of the museum's collections depart every 15 minutes, and are free with admission. The large, open, and noisy main café still manages to be stuffy: a cup of coffee there is more productive of museum fatigue than hours of art-viewing. The bar up above the vast entranceway (open Friday and Saturday, 16.00–20.00) is much more pleasant.

Admission to either the Metropolitan or the Cloisters secures entry to the other, but the sole pleasurable way of visiting both in one day is to look at only one department or one temporary exhibition at the Met in the morning, and then head directly uptown to the Cloisters for the afternoon.

ADDRESS Fifth Avenue (at 82nd Street) New York, NY 10028; (212) 879 5500; www.metmuseum.org
OPEN Sunday, Tuesday to Thursday, 9.30–17.15; Friday, Saturday, 9.30–20.45; roof garden (with bar) open May to October
ADMISSION (suggested, includes Cloisters; see page 7.6) $10; students and seniors $5; free to children under 12 with an adult
DISABILITY ACCESS full (telephone (212) 535 7710, or (212) 879 0421 for the hearing-impaired)
SUBWAY 4, 5, 6 to 86th Street

Museum of the City of New York

Established in 1923, the Museum of the City of New York set out to preserve New York history in the manner of European city museums, such as the Musée Carnavalet in Paris, and others in London, Berlin and Hamburg. Originally relegated to a section of Gracie Mansion, this museum is now housed in its own immense residence on Fifth Avenue. Some 1.5 million objects are held in its collection: of particular importance are its collection of Currier and Ives prints, Jacob Rils photographs, and its theatre department.

Pioneering in its particular attention to the artefacts of material culture, the museum was the first in the country to establish a department dedicated to the preservation and display of toys. Ranging from paintings and dolls' houses to posters and fire engines, the disparate items in the museum's collection are as interesting in relation to each other as they are in their own right. The obscene opulence of the Rockefeller rooms on the top floor, for instance, is thrown into relief by the humble neighbourhood-outreach feel of an ASPCA exhibit on the basement level. While some of the more conventional museum objects on display, such as the furniture pieces, do not offer many original or illuminating insights into New York history, most of the exhibits are more obviously relevant and imaginatively displayed. The Marine gallery, for example, is set up to look like the deck of a ship, and is surrounded by elaborate dioramas, while a recent exhibition, 'New York Toy Stories', used the museum's extensive toy collection to explore the ways that individual, commercial and city histories intersect.

Don't forget to visit the basement floor, which can prove hard to find without a floor-plan. A variety of smaller exhibits there include the People's Hall of Fame, which commemorates individual New Yorkers for their contributions to the city: those honoured include a magic-shop

owner, salsa players and a graffiti artist. The museum's website is worth visiting as well. Like all the best museum web pages, this one uses a sampling technique to treat you to a range of highlights from past and present exhibitions. It also includes exhibitions designed specifically for web-viewing, such as a recent one on nineteenth-century valentines which allowed viewers to see visual details and text that they might have missed in a museum display-case. The museum's educational outreach programmes also take advantage of web technology, with on-line curriculum packets available alongside more traditional offerings.

ADDRESS 1220 Fifth Avenue (at 103rd Street), New York, NY 10029; (212) 534 1672; www.mcny.org
OPEN Wednesday to Saturday, 10.00–17.00; Sunday, 12.00–17.00
ADMISSION (suggested) $5; seniors, students and children $4
DISABILITY ACCESS full
SUBWAY 6 to 103rd Street; 2, 3 to 110th Street

National Academy of Design

The National Academy of Design was founded in 1825 by a group of artists that included Thomas Cole and Rembrandt Peale; its first president was artist and inventor of the telegraph, Samuel F B Morse. For much of the next 100 years, the Academy performed its avowed function of legislating and legitimating the American art scene, while administering a fine arts school based on the academies of Europe. Its annual exhibitions helped to launch the careers of John Frederick Kensett and Jonathan Eastman Johnson, and important paintings of Asher B Durand and Frederic Church debuted there. Other members of the Academy whose works remain in the collections include Eakins, Saint-Gaudens, Homer, and Sargent.

For most of the twentieth century, however, the influence of the National Academy was continually diminishing. Increasingly, the turn-of-the-century Beaux Arts townhouse has become a kind of place-holder for the vestiges of a bygone vision of traditionalist art and art culture. The Academy is thus best visited to view the paintings of the artist members of its heyday.

ADDRESS 1083 Fifth Avenue (at 89th Street), New York, NY 10128; (212) 369- 4880; www.nationalacademy.org
OPEN Wednesday to Sunday, 12.00–17.00
ADMISSION $8; students, seniors and children under 16, $4.50
DISABILITY ACCESS full
SUBWAY 4, 5, 6 to 86th Street

Whitney Museum of American Art

The Whitney was named after its founder, Gertrude Vanderbilt Whitney, a sculptor and patron of the arts. Dedicated to the work of avant-garde artists who had problems exhibiting and selling their work in traditional venues, Whitney believed that collections such as hers would allow new art to thrive and produce a distinctly American artistic vision. She collected a sizable body of this work and offered it to the Met, only to be turned down. Defiantly, she set up her own museum in Greenwich Village in 1930. Unique in its focus on American, rather than European art and in its support of living artists rather than those already canonised, the Whitney was destined to lead a controversial life.

Its current residence on the Upper East Side, for instance, has solicited a steady stream of criticism over the years. Designed by Marcel Breuer and Hamilton Smith, the greyish concrete edifice is shaped like an upside-down staircase with a moat around it and a concrete bridge leading to the entrance. A favourite with art insiders because of its commitment to up-and-coming artists, the Whitney has often been accused of elitism, and its undeniably foreboding façade and moat have been derided by critics as visual evidence of its snobbery. Its Biennial Exhibition has also been the subject of notoriety, serving as the flash-point of the culture wars in the 1980s and early 1990s. The fact that these shows are the only continuous exhibitions to provide an overview of recent artistic developments around the country often goes unnoticed by those put off by the museum's alleged political correctness.

The Whitney also stages important retrospectives of contemporary artists and has canonised several influential artists this way: among the artists to have their first retrospectives there are Jasper Johns and Cindy Sherman. It was also the first museum to present a major exhibition of video. Aside from its forward-looking artistic vision, the Whitney has

Whitney Museum of American Art

a significant permanent collection: this includes the entire artistic estate of Edward Hopper and sizable bodies of work by major figures such as Reginald Marsh, Georgia O'Keefe and Alexander Calder. Its museum-wide 1999–2000 'American Century' show is emblematic of its recent decision to capitalise on the significance of these permanent holdings as a way of securing its place in an increasingly competitive museum world – hopefully this partial jettisoning of its maverick identity won't end up eradicating its current distinctiveness.

ADDRESS 945 Madison Avenue (at 75th Street), New York, NY 10021; (212) 570 3600 (toll-free 1-877-WHITNEY); www.whitney.org
OPEN Tuesday, Wednesday, 11.00–18.00; Thursday, 13.00–20.00 (18.00–20.00 free); Friday to Sunday, 11.00–18.00
ADMISSION $10, students and seniors $8; free to under 12s
DISABILITY ACCESS full (wheelchairs and care chairs available)
SUBWAY 4, 5, 6 to 77th Street

upper west side

African-American Wax and History Museum of Harlem 6.2
American Museum of Natural History 6.6
Cathedral of St John the Divine 6.10
Children's Museum of Manhattan (CMOM) 6.14
Museum of American Folk Art 6.18
New York Historical Society 6.20

African-American Wax and History Museum of Harlem

Some time during your journey from the cherub-covered, brightly painted gateway of this majestic Harlem brownstone, to the dark incense-scented inner hallway plastered with articles about the museum, you'll realise you're in for a unique experience. A peek into the ground-floor room that constitutes the museum reveals an eerie cluster of wax figures, but the uncanny effect is soon dispelled upon the appearance of the museum's captivating tour guide, owner and founder, Raven Chanticleer.

An artist, costume designer and writer, Chanticleer has had a life as varied as his museum collection. Born in Harlem to parents from Barbados and Haiti, he has lived and worked in Texas, Ghana and Paris. The last 20 years have seen him back in Harlem, committed to commemorating the neighbourhood's historical role as a cultural and artistic centre, and a key participant in its current revitalisation. His tour of the museum, then, is at once an autobiography told though the museum's art pieces, a revisionist history of the USA, and a tribute to the diversity of African-American culture. Its highly indiscriminate style is part of the tour's charm – a coconut carving that he made as a child is treated with as much reverence as a painting of the slave trade or a statue of Malcolm X. Virtually everything on display was made by Chanticleer himself, and there is an astonishing range of objects for such a small venue: candles, fertility sticks, sculptures, toys, paintings, voodoo dolls, as well as the wax sculptures themselves. These are definitely the highlight of the tour, and are introduced as if they were intimate friends of the owner. Unexpected juxtapositions abound, as you move from Harriet Tubman to Lady Day, David Dinkins to Magic Johnson. There is also a wax Madonna (the pop star, not the Virgin) in blackface and

a startlingly convincing likeness of the owner himself. The tour continues outside, where statues and sculptures are scattered around in a cheerfully haphazard fashion. Here, open-air art workshops are often held for school tours. The museum is especially child-friendly, and younger visitors are encouraged to engage in art, as well as to learn about its ability to embody history.

ADDRESS 316 West 115th Street (between Manhattan Avenue and Frederick Douglass Boulevard), New York, NY 10026–2308; (212) 678 7818
OPEN Tuesday to Sunday, 13.00–18.00 (by appointment only)
ADMISSION adults and children over ten $10; children under ten $5; group rates available
DISABILITY ACCESS none
SUBWAY B, C to 116th Street

upper west side

American Museum of Natural History

Founded in 1869 by Albert Bickmore, the Museum of Natural History took up residence on its current vast estate on Central Park West in 1874. It has since expanded to encompass 23 buildings altogether, including the Rose Center for Earth and Space (formerly the Hayden Planetarium). Apart from amassing a collection of objects relating to natural history, the museum sponsors scientific expeditions, serves as a centre of scientific research for over 200 scientists, and disseminates scientific knowledge through its periodicals and public education forums.

Natural history is understood by the museum as the history of 'life on Earth, as well as evidence of what we know about the universe beyond our planet'. This broad, all-encompassing definition, together with the vastness of the museum's holdings, leads to some serious curatorial challenges. Even though the museum only displays about two per cent of its collection at any given time, the number and diversity of its displays require more of a user-friendly format than the institution provides; large parts of it are not well signed and consequently feel unwieldy and overwhelming. Though the museum is carrying out extensive renovations, it is obviously too large to redo all at once and some exhibits remain egregiously out-of-date. The anthropological sections are particularly fusty, with some embarrassingly reductive cultural exhibits still in place. Mouldy and uncontextualised mammal displays, which dominate the first two floors, also cry out for renewal.

The new exhibits are a joy by comparison. On the fourth floor, an orientation centre provides viewers with an excellent informational overview of the prehistoric rooms, and suggests paths between the exhibits. The displays here and in other recently added permanent rooms such as the Hall of Biodiversity, are aesthetically lively and effec-

American Museum of Natural History

tively educational, with up-to-date information presented so as to appeal to both adults and children. Recent temporary exhibitions, such as one on Haitian voodoo, have been equally successful, hailed by critics as innovative and intelligent. We can only hope that the museum manages to renovate the majority of its exhibits before the sections which have already been updated begin to look obsolete all over again.

ADDRESS Central Park West (at 79th Street), New York, NY 10024;
(212) 769 5100; www.amnh.org
OPEN Sunday to Thursday, 10.00–17.45; Friday, Saturday, 10.00–20.45
ADMISSION (suggested) $9.50; students and seniors $7.50; children $6
DISABILITY ACCESS full
SUBWAY B, C to 81st Street

Cathedral of St John the Divine

While not strictly a museum, the seat of the Episcopal Diocese of New York is an impressive monument to Gothic architecture and is chock-full of religious art, both old and new. Begun in 1892 and built almost exclusively out of hand-carved granite and limestone, the cathedral claims to be the largest in the world, though it is still a work in progress: its arms were never finished. (And because its stonemasonry programme is in hiatus due to lack of funding, the date of its eventual completion remains undetermined.) A spectacular building, its massive solid stone arches and buttresses manage to avoid the heaviness of some Gothic architecture, and feel at once delicate and majestic. Moreover, the pleasing uniformity of the structure serves as a complement to the wide range of artistic influences that it houses.

As the banner to multiculturalism hanging in the nave indicates, the cathedral is dedicated to acknowledging and celebrating a diversity of religious beliefs and subjecting Christian tenets to the most progressive and inclusive of interpretations. Thus the medical chapel contains tributes to those who have died of AIDS, and the chapel of St Savior, alongside more traditional religious art, boasts a handsome metallic Keith Haring altarpiece. Contemporary art by local artists and students is dispersed throughout the chapel and visitors are encouraged to add their own contributions to the Muriel Rukeyser poetry wall. The vertical tour offers a bird's-eye view of the cathedral's exemplary architecture. After climbing 124 feet of spiral staircase, visitors find themselves near the roof of the building, where they can examine the windows in detail and walk on a flying buttress.

To the side of the cathedral, its Biblical and Hope Rose Gardens are also worth a visit – they contain herbs, flowers and a number of elusive free-roaming peacocks. In addition to its intense involvement with a

Cathedral of St John the Divine

number of community outreach and school programmes, the cathedral offers medieval arts workshops, public concerts, performances and art exhibitions.

ADDRESS 1047 Amsterdam Avenue
(at 112th Street), New York, NY 10025;
(212) 316 7540;
www.stjohndivine.org/cathedral
OPEN 7.30–18.00
OPEN TO TOURISTS Tuesday to Saturday,
9.00–17.00
PUBLIC TOURS Tuesday to Saturday, 11.00;
Sunday, 13.00;
reservations on (212) 932 7347
ADMISSION $3
DISABILITY ACCESS limited
SUBWAY 1, 9 to Cathedral Parkway

Children's Museum of Manhattan (CMOM)

Though not as engaging as its precursor, the Brooklyn Children's Museum (see page 9.2), CMOM will still appeal to younger children: and it's just big enough that you can probably get through it all before your small child gets cranky. Explicitly geared towards ages 0 to 10, the museum – originally founded in 1973 – offers a range of exhibits and activities designed to expose children to literature, the arts, and media and communications. Small wonder, then, that picture-book-related exhibits are all the rage here. When I visited, there was a walk-though version of Maira Kalman's book, *Max (A Dog)*, a room devoted to John Lennon's book for his son Sean, a Seuss gallery (filled with original sketches for his books) and an extremely popular Seuss playhouse.

Most of the exhibitions are designed to teach through interaction. In the recent 'Body Odyssey', for instance, children learn about the digestive system by crawling through a giant mouth and small intestines, and play video-games where they fight off invading germs. Workshops offered several times a day are designed to complement the special exhibits, reflecting the museum's commitment to providing children with multiple approaches to learning. Thus, installations in 'Body Odyssey' about the healing power of scabs were paired with workshops in which participants made simulated scabs out of craft materials. By developing an appreciation of the delicate structure of scabs (and revelling in the ickyness of it all), young visitors are engagingly reminded of the exhibit's lesson not to pick them.

For children at the older end of the target spectrum, the museum's most compelling activity is probably the Time Warner Media Center, where they can participate in workshops on TV production. Though Time Warner's sponsorship of the programme provokes the suspicion

that its young visitors are learning as much about consumption as production, the workshops enable them to handle and learn to use equipment not usually readily available elsewhere, such as TV cameras, control monitors and sound and editing equipment.

In an outdoor area towards the back of the museum, the Urban Tree House provides interactive lessons about recycling and its role in preserving the environment. Perhaps the best aspect of CMOM is its popular and well executed daily activity schedule. Jam-packed, dizzyingly energetic events – including dance, art, music and storytelling workshops – occur at regular intervals and are open to both children and their parents.

ADDRESS The Tisch Building, 212 West 83rd Street, New York, NY 10024; (212) 721 1234; www.cmom.org
OPEN Wednesday to Sunday, 10.00–17.00
ADMISSION $6; seniors $3.00; free for children under one; group rates available
DISABILITY ACCESS full
SUBWAY 1, 9, B or C to 86th Street

Children's Museum of Manhattan (CMOM)

upper west side

Museum of American Folk Art

If, like me, you have an allergy to all things quaint (and particularly to that peculiar blend of the puritanical and the sentimental that is the American version), visit the Museum of American Folk Art. For where else can you find the rich diversity that is American folk art integrated without recourse to conceptions of American and folk that are at once problematical and bland?

The exhibition of the museum's permanent collection, America's Heritage, opens up questions that most exhibitions of American folk art try to elude, such as the influence of European, African, and Native American culture, the continuity or discontinuity between regions and historical periods, and the mutual influence between vernacular, popular, and high art. The permanent exhibition is broken up into intelligently curated displays, each of which examines a specific theme or set of problems. Here are collected a number of splendid pieces, mostly from the eighteenth and nineteenth centuries – among them whirligigs, portraits, landscapes, furniture, textiles, weathervanes, trinket boxes, sketchbooks, and decoys. The collection of quilts is exceptional.

After opening in 1963, the museum moved to its present location opposite Lincoln Center in 1989. In 2001, while maintaining its current galleries, the museum will quadruple its floor space by opening an ambitious new building opposite MOMA and the American Craft Museum.

ADDRESS Two Lincoln Square, New York, NY 10023; (212) 595 9533; www.folkartmuse.org
OPEN Tuesday to Sunday, 11.30–19.30
ADMISSION free
DISABILITY ACCESS full
SUBWAY 1, 9 to 66th Street; A, B, C, D to 59th Street/Columbus Circle

...E ALSO SHALL DW...
...ALL LIE DOWN WITH THE L...
...EATLING TOGETHER; AND A L...
Isaiah 11:6...

New York Historical Society

A group of New York politicians and professionals founded the New York Historical Society in 1804, when the project of constructing an American national history was in its earliest stages. Now housed in a 1904 neo-classical building on Central Park West, the Society remains largely privately funded, and maintains a dual focus on national and local history. While large-scale temporary exhibitions sometimes focus on national historical figures like George Washington, they often treat a wide variety of more localised topics, from the history of the New York City Ballet to that of New York's police force.

The permanent collections are astonishing for their range and depth. The Luman Reed Gallery displays a massive collection of European and American works of art from the Colonial period to the early twentieth century, including paintings by Thomas Cole, folk sculpture, and John James Audubon's 431 watercolours for *The Birds of America*. The institution also holds an important collection of photographs, including many daguerreotypes and early views of the city, as well as Matthew Brady's Civil War photographs. The architectural collection includes the contents of the offices of McKim, Mead & White, architects of many of New York's major museums. And this is to say nothing of the library, or of the institution's vast holdings of decorative arts and ephemera.

ADDRESS 2 West 77th Street (at Central Park West), New York, NY 10024; (212) 873 3400; www.nyhistory.org

OPEN Tuesday to Sunday, 11.00–17.00 (museum and gallery; print room by appointment only)

ADMISSION $5; seniors and children $3

DISABILITY ACCESS limited

SUBWAY B, C to 81st Street

upper manhattan

American Numismatic Society 7.2
Children's Museum of the Native American 7.4
The Cloisters 7.6
Dyckman Farmhouse Museum 7.8
Hispanic Society of America 7.10
Morris-Jumel Mansion 7.14
The Studio Museum in Harlem 7.18

American Numismatic Society

The formation of the American Numismatic Society in 1858 is related both to the flourishing of learned societies in the USA in the late nineteenth century, and to the discovery and mining of gold in California that same year. The latter resulted in federal coinage reforms that produced coins of new size and shape for the first time in half a century. Correspondences such as these, which illuminate the extensive interrelation between the history of coinage and that of commerce, politics, technology and culture, are insightfully drawn out in the institution's permanent exhibition, 'The World of Coins'. Because of this diversity of approaches, the exhibition avoids the tediousness of the grand overview, despite the ambitious scope of its 3000-year history of coinage. Thus, while the Society's exceptional library, as well as some of its less ambitious exhibits, are of interest only to the scholar or serious collector, the American Numismatic Society elicits surprisingly broad appeal.

The Society represents the foremost collection of coins, medals, and paper money in the USA, though the two public galleries display only about 2000 objects. Since the early 1980s the institution has sponsored a steady schedule of public programmes, including conferences and lectures. It's best to 'phone ahead, since the Society is scheduled to move downtown from its present location in the Audubon Terrace Complex to 140 William Street before the end of the year 2000.

ADDRESS Audubon Terrace, Broadway at 155th Street, New York, NY 10032; (212) 234 3130; www.amnumsoc2.org
OPEN Tuesday to Saturday, 9.00–16.30; Sunday, 13.00–16.00
ADMISSION free
DISABILITY ACCESS none
SUBWAY 1 to 157th Street

Children's Museum of the Native American

Essentially a museum for school groups, the Children's Museum of the Native American is highly interactive and performance-oriented. The only permanent exhibition consists of the famous photographs of Indians taken at the turn of the century by Edward S Curtis. Visiting children take part in a two-hour programme that begins with a hands-on demonstration of Hopi, Pueblo, and Apache modes of cooking, shelter-building, and craft-making. After a puppet show that depicts the myths and legends of Southwest Indians, children gather around an Indian drum to sing chants, play Indian games, and even learn Navajo sign language. At the end of the routine, visitors can buy tomahawks, beaded necklaces, and Indian dolls from costumed staff at the 'trading post'.

In the hope of treating the varieties of Native American cultures within the USA with some degree of specificity, the museum emphasises the culture of a different Native American region each year.

ADDRESS 550 West 155th Street, New York, NY 10032; (212) 283 1122
OPEN Monday to Friday, 10.00–13.00 (by appointment)
ADMISSION $4
DISABILITY ACCESS none
SUBWAY 1, 9 to 157th Street

The Cloisters

Before the Metropolitan Museum took over this stunning collection in 1926, aided by a Rockefeller donation, the American artist George Grey Barnard had assembled its various parts from Romanesque and Gothic cloisters in France. Textiles (including the famous 'Unicorn' tapestries), icons, stained glass and window arches, centuries apart in origin, are placed side by side, forming what can appear to be an inharmonious hodge-podge. A staircase, taken from 'a courtyard at 29, rue de la Tannerie, Abbeville', and stuck into a corner leading nowhere, calls to mind, jarringly, how far it has travelled from its original context. In one cloister, the architectural components of half of a Languedoc cloister join Lyonnais columns and freestanding marble figures from Tuscany. At the same time, however, the museum's elegant use of the cloister design functions as an organising principle that connects the museum's disparate elements.

One of the Cloisters' most charming features is the exterior courtyard, which is filled with plants favoured in the medieval era, such as quince and pomegranate trees, medicinal herbs, and olive bushes. The peacefulness of the gardens is complemented by the surrounding tranquillity of Fort Tryon Park, donated to the city by John D Rockefeller Jr. Rockefeller also managed to secure the view across the river by purchasing 700 acres of land behind the New Jersey Palisades.

ADDRESS Fort Tryon Park, New York, NY 10040; (212) 923 3700
OPEN Tuesday to Sunday, 9.30–17.15 (November to February, 9.30–16.45)
ADMISSION (suggested, includes same-day admission to the Met) $10; students and seniors $5; free to children under 12 with an adult
DISABILITY ACCESS limited
SUBWAY A to 190th Street; then take M4 bus one stop

The Cloisters

upper manhattan

Dyckman Farmhouse Museum

A short walk away from the Cloisters and Inwood Hill Park, the white clapboard walls and tidy, fussy grounds of the Dyckman house are strikingly at odds with the starkly urban landscape around it. Once a 450-acre estate and one of the largest farmholdings in the area, this is the city's last colonial farmhouse. Photographs and artefacts from the eighteenth and nineteenth century in the museum's Relic Room help you to visualise this remote-seeming period of Inwood history.

Built by William Dyckman in 1784 after the original seventeenth-century home had been destroyed by Revolutionary soldiers, the house is a good example of the Dutch-American style of the period. If you're at all familiar with the sparse and gloomy decor of eighteenth-century farmhouses, you won't be surprised by much in its interior. Furniture, porcelain, and other household accoutrements from the last two centuries – such as cooking implements and a wooden cradle – are set up inside to evoke the lifestyles of its former inhabitants. The most interesting relic among a number of commonplace ones is a 'Nine Man Morris' gameboard carved into the stone next to the kitchen. It is presumed to have been created and played with by the Dyckman children but the details of its use remain obscure. A tour of the grounds reveals an old-fashioned kitchen garden and a replica of a Hessian officer's hut, built in 1917 to evoke the shelters that soldiers built in the area during the Revolution.

ADDRESS 4881 Broadway (at 204th Street), New York, NY 10034; (212) 304 9422
OPEN Tuesday to Sunday, 11.00–16.00
ADMISSION free (donations appreciated)
DISABILITY ACCESS none
SUBWAY A to 207th Street

Hispanic Society of America

No less than the Frick Collection or the Morgan Library, this institution retains the form and feel given to it by its founder, Archer Milton Huntington, in 1904. The vast majority of pieces now on display had already been amassed by Huntington when the museum opened its doors to the public in 1908. Everywhere the institution reflects Huntington's patronage of and friendships with the Spanish expatriate artists and intellectuals who made up 'the generation of '98', many of whom are depicted in portraits in the reading room. The most important of these relationships was with the painter Joaquín Sorolla y Bastida, whose monumental series *The Provinces of Spain* covers the walls of the west wing. Another friend, the poet Juan-Ramon Jiménez, was asked to scrawl an inscription on a column of the gorgeous central room, which was designed to resemble a Spanish-Baroque courtyard.

Both the inefficient form of this room and the lack of display space bring new meaning to the phrase 'an embarrassment of riches'. The Pietà of El Greco and three important portraits by Velázquez are hung a little too high, in order to accommodate beneath them a large, stunning display of Hispano-Muslim lustreware, and the light that so beautifully bathes the tiles of the floor below sheds glare on the paintings. Display cases for decorative art are tucked underneath Hispano-Muslim brocades and Renaissance liturgical vestments, while archaeological artefacts are spread among the artworks. This clutter makes for considerable charm as well as confusion, however, and contrasts sharply with the hyper-rationalised gallery space of New York's more up-to-date museums.

While the overwhelming majority of artworks on display are Spanish, the holdings of jewellery, *ars sacra*, ceramics, and works in gold and silver include pieces from Latin America, Portugal, and the Philippines. The

library, too, holds a rich collection of documents relating to Latin America's colonial period, including a 1526 map of the world by Juan Vespucci and catechisms in several Amerindian languages. Both the sparseness of Latin American art and the crowding of the display space are likely to be remedied when the Society expands into the neighbouring space of the former Museum of the American Indian in 2004.

ADDRESS Audubon Terrace, 613 West 155th Street (at Broadway), New York, NY 10032; (212) 926 2234; www.hispanicsociety.org
OPEN Tuesday to Saturday, 10.00–16.30; Sunday, 13.00–16.00
ADMISSION free
DISABILITY ACCESS none
SUBWAY 1 to 157th Street

Morris-Jumel Mansion

British Colonel Roger Morris built this Palladian-style Georgian villa as a summer home in 1765. At the time, it was ten miles north from the City of New York, located on a 130-acre estate that stretched between the Hudson and Harlem Rivers. After the loyalist Morris returned to England during the Revolutionary War, George Washington briefly made the house his military headquarters. The mansion became a summer home again when Stephen and Eliza Jumel acquired it in 1810. The Jumels added gardens, stained glass, gilt-framed mirrors and colourful French Empire furnishings. These elements contrast sharply with the spartan character of George Washington's restored bedroom and study. After the death of her husband, Eliza Jumel became an enormously successful real-estate entrepreneur, and was one of the wealthiest women in New York by mid-century. She was briefly married to ex-Vice President Aaron Burr, and died in 1865, when the borders of New York City were approaching the mansion's location in northern Manhattan.

The oldest remaining house in Manhattan, the Morris-Jumel Mansion is also one of the most compelling of New York's antiquarian house museums. When the house was built, both the octagonal rear wing and the grand two-storey portico with colossal columns were unprecedented in American architecture. The dressing room and dining room were also rare features, even among houses of the colonial gentry. In the arrangement of furnishings and artefacts, the curators have meticulously created a model for the stewardship of period homes. The arrangement of the salon looks strange, for instance, because much of the furniture is placed against the walls, as it was when not in use during the Colonial period.

The signage and a short, informative video document eighteenth-century modes of dining and entertaining, and scrupulously detail the

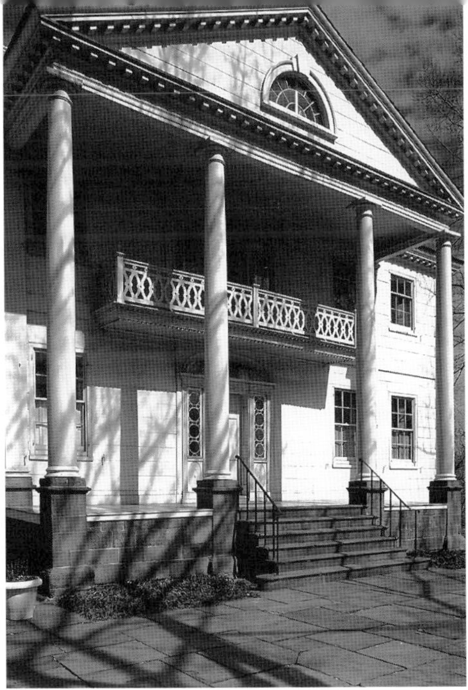

process of restoration. The commanding hillside perspective that successively enabled the Palladian vision of the country gentleman and the vision of military scouts now affords picnicking visitors a pleasant view over Harlem from the mansion's lawn.

ADDRESS 65 Jumel Terrace (between 160th and 162nd Streets), New York, NY 10032; (212) 923 8008
OPEN Wednesday to Sunday, 10.00–16.00
ADMISSION $3; students and seniors $2
DISABILITY ACCESS limited (telephone in advance)
SUBWAY C to 163rd Street

The Studio Museum in Harlem

Though the Studio Museum's minimalist white gallery spaces bespeak a 'neutral' modernist outlook on the art housed there, the museum firmly believes in the value of dialogue and context. This approach, together with the museum's unique focus on both African-American art and that of the African diaspora, has led to a number of pioneering exhibitions, such as its 1997–98 show 'Transforming the Crown: African, Asian and Caribbean Artists in Britain, 1966–1996'.

Opened in 1968 as a studio and temporary exhibition space, a central component of its mission is the revision of traditional notions of modernist art to include African-Americans whose work has been over-looked or undervalued – a 1998 museum publication on the work of Norman Lewis re-framed his work in the context of American abstract expressionism. The museum continues to offer artists studio and work-shop space; an annual Artists-in-Residence programme involves three emerging artists of African descent. Its educational programmes include the Cooperative School Program, which places artists in Harlem schools, an art education programme that targets at-risk youths, and classes on the art of collecting. The new 5200-square-foot sculpture garden is the first to be dedicated to artists of African descent. Further expansions will include more gallery space, an atrium, an auditorium, and a café.

ADDRESS 144 West 125th Street (between Lenox and Seventh Avenues), New York, NY 10027; (212) 864 4500; www.StudioMuseum.org
OPEN Wednesday to Friday, 10.00–17.00; Saturday and Sunday, 13.00–18.00
ADMISSION $5; seniors and students $3; children under 12 $1.00
DISABILITY ACCESS full
SUBWAY A, B, C, D, 2, 3, 4, 5, 6 to 125th Street

bronx

Bronx Museum of the Arts   8.2
Edgar Allan Poe Cottage   8.4

Bronx Museum of the Arts

This museum's collection is as contemporary as the design of its building, an extensively renovated former synagogue. Though smaller than some of the other borough museums in New York, the Bronx Museum makes up in energy and vision what it might lack in size and resources. Founded in 1971 by local residents, it is explicitly devoted to the surrounding neighbourhood and the culturally diverse population that resides there; its permanent collection highlights the work of artists of African, Asian and Latin American ancestry. One of its earliest major exhibitions, 'Devastation/Resurrection: The South Bronx', set the tone for the museum's project. While refusing to ignore the continuing socio-economic problems that the neighbourhood faces, the museum uses cross-cultural dialogue to meet the challenges of renewal. Innovative exhibitions, inclusive of an extraordinarily wide range of media, strive to acknowledge and include genres typically overlooked by more traditional museums, such as graffiti art and rap music.

The Art and Media School functions as an extension of the exhibition space. Student art is on display alongside other shows, and you can often see the school's many classes in fine art, computer graphics, and video in session as you walk through the museum's lower level. A conference room on the second floor houses a variety of music and art demonstrations, workshops and other community-based activities.

ADDRESS 1040 Grand Concourse, Bronx, NY 10456; (718) 681 6000
OPEN Wednesday, 15.00–21.00; Thursday, Friday, 10.00–17.00;
Saturday, Sunday, 13.00–18.00
ADMISSION (suggested) $3; students $2; seniors $1.00; children under 12 free
DISABILITY ACCESS full
SUBWAY C, D or 4 to 161st Street

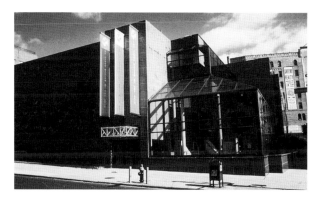

Edgar Allan Poe Cottage

In 1846, seeking a retreat from the whirlwind of lower Manhattan, and anxious about the worsening tubercular condition of his wife Virginia, Poe moved with his wife and his mother-in-law Maria Clemm to this rural single-storey farmhouse. Virginia died a year later, bequeathing to generations of high-school teachers an explanation for Poe's obsession with death. Poe stayed on in the cottage until he died during a visit to Baltimore in 1849. (This is about all he did in Baltimore, despite the common association of Poe with that city.) Many of Poe's most important poems and stories were written in the house's attic, including 'Eureka', 'The Bells', and 'Annabel Lee'. Several, like 'Landor's Cottage' and 'The Domain of Arnheim', feature landscape descriptions culled from the area surrounding the cottage, especially what is now the New York Botanical Garden.

Most of the cottage has been restored to resemble its state when Poe lived here. Period pieces complement furniture remaining from Poe's time, but it's not obvious, even for the most ardent Poe enthusiast, what to do once you get there. (Touch his bed?) You can watch an informative video focusing on Poe's years in the cottage, but the attic room in which Poe did much of his writing remains virtually empty. The Bronx County Historical Society, which superintends the museum, is in the process of adding more artefacts and signage. The 1812 house may also be of interest as an example of a modest early nineteenth-century home.

ADDRESS Grand Concourseand East Kingsbridge Road, Bronx, NY 10458; (718) 881 8900
OPEN Saturday, 10.00–16.00; Sunday, 13.00–17.00t
ADMISSION $2 DISABILITY ACCESS none
SUBWAY D, 4 to Kingsbridge Road

brooklyn

Brooklyn Children's Museum 9.2
Brooklyn Historical Society 9.6
Brooklyn Museum of Art (BMA) 9.8
The Kurdish Library and Museum 9.12
New York Transit Museum 9.14

Brooklyn Children's Museum

Assemble an 8-foot-high elephant skeleton puzzle, play musical instruments from around the world, or pet a snake from the live animal collection! From the beginning of its 100-year history as the world's first museum for children, the emphasis at Brooklyn Children's has been on engaging the participation of its young visitors. The museum is so playful, so gratuitously colourful, and so highly interactive that it requires an extraordinary level of restraint on the part of any adult visitors who don't want to be seen climbing, crawling, giggling, and responding aloud to the displays. Even in the exhibits behind glass cases, children activate sounds and lights, flip signage cards, and compare objects through sight, sound, and smell.

In the permanent exhibition 'The Mystery of Things', visitors are invited to re-examine the world of banal household objects. Elsewhere, the museum exposes children to more unaccustomed sights, including a broadly international collection of sculpture, masks, costumes, ceremonial objects, and, of course, toys. A sizable natural history collection is displayed in a variety of exhibits that teach children about biology and ecology in the most interactive and accessible manner, without dumbing-down or proselytising.

The majority of exhibits are curated to accommodate undirected play and learning by children of varying ages, interests and aptitudes. In an exhibition of musical instruments, for example, it's left up to the individual visitor to decide whether he or she wants to explore the musical or the cultural significance of the instruments on display, or just beat on the drums, xylophones, and thumb-pianos. At the same time, the extraordinarily animated and patient staff give live-animal presentations, tell stories, and direct special projects. The Brooklyn Children's Museum pioneered the very idea of a children's museum, and its emphasis on the

Brooklyn Children's Museum

interactive has had a huge influence on the city's other children's museums (Manhattan and Staten Island). Similarly, the BCM sponsors a series of educational programmes that have been held up as models of community outreach.

Unfortunately, the Brooklyn Children's Museum is not visited as often as it might be by Manhattanites, as it is located out in the neighbourhood of Crown Heights. Even if you're coming from Upper Manhattan, however, it's worth the trip.

ADDRESS 145 Brooklyn Avenue, Brooklyn, NY 11213; (718) 735 4400; www.bchildmus.org
OPEN Wednesday to Friday, 14.00–17.00; Saturday, Sunday and most school holidays, 10.00–17.00
ADMISSION (suggested) $3
DISABILITY ACCESS full
SUBWAY 3, C, A to Kingston Avenue; free trolley shuttle service from Grand Army Plaza hourly from 10.15 to 16.15 on Saturday and Sunday

Brooklyn Historical Society

Founded in 1863 as the Long Island Historical Society, the Brooklyn Historical Society remains in the stately red-brick and terracotta building that George B Post designed for it in 1881. However, the Brooklyn Heights institution now prides itself on being less stodgy and more responsive to the borough's diversity than its founders were. Temporary exhibitions draw on the Society's collection of eighteenth-century furniture, paintings, prints, photographs, and memorabilia. A variety of permanent exhibits focus on the Brooklyn Dodgers, Brooklyn Bridge, Coney Island, and Brooklyn Navy Yard. On the second floor, the library holds historical documents and books by and about Brooklyn inhabitants, and serves as a resource for both scholars and Brooklynites interested in the history of their respective neighbourhoods.

The Society sponsors educational programmes, in-house publications, and after-school art workshops; it also runs an impressive website that supports a digital gallery of 30,000 images and includes exhibits designed specifically for the web. Currently in the process of a $10-million renovation that will allow for the display of the expanding permanent collections, the Society continues to offer public programmes. Its galleries and library are scheduled to reopen in 2001.

ADDRESS 128 Pierrepont Street, Brooklyn, NY 11202; (718) 624 0890
OPEN Tuesday to Saturday, 12.00–17.00
ADMISSION $2.50; seniors and children $1
DISABILITY ACCESS full
SUBWAY 2, 3, 4, 5 to Borough Hall; A, F to Jay Street; R, M to Court Street

Brooklyn Museum of Art (BMA)

It may be that those features of this museum which made it most compelling during its extended period of formation are precisely those that make it less so now. Established in 1933, the BMA claims a heritage that goes back to 1823, when Brooklyn's first free circulating library was founded to cater to the distinctively working-class nature of Brooklyn's population. This localised focus originated in the days before Brooklyn had become part of New York and has been maintained to the present day, though it seems less warranted now. Despite my own stock of Brooklyn petty nationalism, I was unable to access what was distinctive or coherent about a contemporary-art series called 'Working in Brooklyn'.

The emphasis on Brooklyn, however, did not prevent the BMA from amassing an encyclopedic collection, which the visitor is prepared for by the granite façade of Charles McKim's imposing 1897 neo-classical building, deeply engraved with the names of great artists. Except for a magnificent room of 58 Rodin sculptures and a substantial display of nineteenth-century French and American painting, the curators seem to have scrupulously avoided acquiring too much of anything in particular, as though specific emphases would have betrayed a lack of objectivity. Consequently, it's difficult to make an afternoon out of a visit to a particular department, as one can do at the Met. Along with the lack of air-conditioning on the top floor, this can make for museum fatigue rather quickly, sending the visitor to seek refuge in the complex of nineteenth-century parks and gardens that surround the museum.

Having said that, the museum does possess an enormous collection of extraordinary artworks. In addition to European and American painting and sculpture, the museum has strong collections of Arabic, Egyptian, Native American, Latin American, and Asian art. Moreover,

brooklyn

Brooklyn Museum of Art (BMA)

the BMA was very early in displaying its considerable holdings of African art on aesthetic rather than anthropological grounds. The temporary shows tend to be more energetically curated than the museum's permanent collection, and feature artists range from Mariko Mori to Albert Pinkham Ryder.

ADDRESS 200 Eastern Parkway, Brooklyn, NY 11238; (718) 638 5000; www.brooklynart.org
OPEN Wednesday to Friday, 10.00–17.00; Saturday, Sunday, 11.00–18.00; first Saturday of month, 11.00–23.00
ADMISSION $4; students $2; seniors $1.50; free to children under 12 with an adult
DISABILITY ACCESS full
SUBWAY 2, 3 to Eastern Parkway/Brooklyn Museum

The Kurdish Library and Museum

Located in a privately owned brownstone in Brooklyn, the tiny, delightful Kurdish Library and Museum dovetails with the life and home of its proprietress, a charismatic scholar and raconteuse who started the collection with a single book and headdress left to her by her late Kurdish husband. The collections grew in large part through the donations of artefacts by Kurds from all over the world. Now the Kurdish Library holds 2000 volumes on Kurdish history and culture, mostly in Kurdish and English. The significance of the artefacts on display, including musical instruments, rugs, and traditional costumes, is amplified by the curator's recounting of her personal relation to them.

Downstairs, the library provides a haven for scholarly researchers. Holdings include periodicals, photographs, and video and audio cassettes.

ADDRESS 144 Underhill Avenue (at Park Place), Brooklyn, NY 11238; (718) 783 7930
OPEN Monday to Thursday, 10.00–15.00 (appointment recommended)
ADMISSION free
DISABILITY ACCESS none
SUBWAY D, Q to 7th Avenue; 2, 3 to Grand Army Plaza

New York Transit Museum

Occupying an ex-subway station from the 1930s, the New York Transit Museum cuts a wide swath through New York's public-transit history from the turn of the century to the present. The visitor begins by learning about early labour conditions and construction methods, and moves on to consider technological advances and debates over public services. Arte-facts include samples of the distinctive tile mosaics of New York subway stations, turnstiles, signage, fare boxes, subway maps, a signal tower, and even a recorded sample of New York's typically incomprehensible train delay announcements.

A series of 20 restored subway cars from 1904 to 1967 are lined up on two tracks. These cars' wicker seats, ceiling fans, concrete floors, and period advertisements truly give one the impression of having entered another era. Now that New York trains are relatively graffiti-proof, they should consider adding a car from a D-train of the early '80s.

ADDRESS corner of Boerum Place and Schermerhorn Street, Brooklyn, NY 11201; (718) 243 8601; www.mta.nyc.ny.us
OPEN Tuesday to Friday, 10.00–16.00; Saturday, Sunday, 12.00–17.00
ADMISSION $3
DISABILITY ACCESS full
SUBWAY 2, 3, 4, 5 to Borough Hall; M, N, R, to Court Street; A, C, G to Hoyt-Schermerhorn; A, C,F to Jay Street/Borough Hall

queens

American Museum of the Moving Image (AMMI) 10.2
The Isamu Noguchi Garden Museum 10.6
New York Hall of Science 10.8
PS1 Contemporary Art Center 10.12
Queens Museum of Art 10.16

American Museum of the Moving Image (AMMI)

AMMI grew out of efforts to save the Astoria Studios, which had been built by Paramount in 1920 but had slowly declined as Hollywood ascended. Amid efforts to bring film production back to New York, the museum opened to the public in 1988. The permanent exhibition, 'Behind the Screen', traces the history of moving image technology from the days of early cinema to the present, from the Lumière brothers to computer animation, and from your grandparents' television to Lara Croft.

The most fascinating part of the museum consists of several interactive stations, where visitors learn how to dub speaking parts, make a 30-second animated film, edit soundtracks, and create special effects. As part of the museum's historical function, one of these stations and several aspects of the exhibition illuminate early cinema techniques in a truly accessible and entertaining fashion. But the focus of the exhibition extends broadly beyond the technology of production; the collections also include a great number of antique movie posters, fan memorabilia, and artefacts documenting the distribution and exhibition of the moving image. (These latter facets might be more compelling if the relationship between them and the elements of film production were investigated more closely.)

AMMI is already very much engaged with new digital media, and with the question of how digital technology will retrospectively alter our sense of the history of the moving image. The museum runs a continuing seminar series on digital media, and a long-term interactive exhibition chronicles the history of the video arcade game. (In other words, you get to play Pong and Asteroids.) Check the newspaper before you come out to Queens, since films run daily in several

American Museum of the Moving Image (AMMI)

screening rooms – among these *Tut's Fever*, a hokey and loving homage to the neo-Egyptian movie houses of the 1920s. Because of the museum's broad focus on American cinema, the film programming is generally less obscure and arty than in the city's other venues for repertory cinema.

ADDRESS 3601 35th Avenue (at 36th Street), Astoria, NY 11106; (718) 784 4520; www.ammi.org
OPEN Tuesday to Friday, 12.00–17.00; Saturday, Sunday, 11.00–18.00
ADMISSION $8.50; students and seniors $5.50; children $4.50
DISABILITY ACCESS full
SUBWAY R, G to Steinway Street

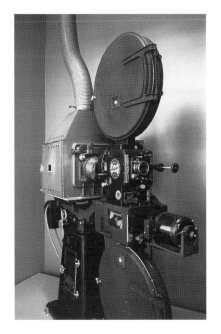

The Isamu Noguchi Garden Museum

Noguchi took over an abandoned photoengraving plant in the mid 1970s, and converted it into an office, studio, and storage space for artworks. Ten years later Noguchi and architect Shoji Sadao expanded the building, installed pieces from more than 60 years of his career, and opened the present museum. The collection includes not only sculpture, but also photographs of Noguchi's large-scale public projects and videos of performances on stage sets that he designed for choreographer Martha Graham.

The space has a pristine quality, both in the sun-bathed maple of the upstairs gallery, and in the indoor/outdoor gallery, where the exposed steel beams, concrete-block, brick walls, and metal ceilings of the photoengraving plant remain. Though over 250 pieces are arranged in roughly chronological order, the unassuming presence of the galleries provides a route through the work that never feels forced or didactic; Noguchi's self-made basalt tombstone blends in inconspicuously with similar late works in the sculpture garden. The dual nature of the garden and museum is echoed throughout, in the complex interplay between interior and exterior. The galleries offer several views and exits into the garden, and the industrial quality of the indoor/outdoor galleries echoes the character of the surrounding neighbourhood. These latter are open to rain, snow, and even the invasion of small birch trees, just as several of the indoor sculptures contain water and fragments of vegetal life.

ADDRESS 32–37 Vernon Boulevard, Long Island City (Queens), NY 11106; (718) 721 1932; www.noguchi.org
OPEN April to October, Wednesday to Friday, 10.00–17.00; Saturday, Sunday, 11.00–18.00
ADMISSION $4; students and seniors $2 DISABILITY ACCESS limited
SUBWAY N to Broadway in Queens

queens

New York Hall of Science

The New York Hall of Science began life as an exhibition in the 1964 World's Fair, and its current incarnation manages to retain some of the excitement and energy of that occasion, a few architectural remnants of which are still visible in surrounding Corona Park. Taking advantage of its position as the only science museum in New York City, and of its growing popularity, the museum has expanded exponentially over the last few years, and is planning to double in size again by 2004. Though adults will not be bored here, this museum, like almost all science museums, is pedagogical in aim and geared mainly towards children. The exhibits have been thoughtfully arranged to appeal to a wide range of age groups, however, and even the youngest child's needs and interests have been anticipated.

Devoted to the idea that hands-on experience is the best tool of learning, the museum has an extensive collection of interactive exhibits. Consequently, what seems like a small space actually takes a decent amount of time to cover. Most of the exhibits operate as follows: you participate in an activity, watch a neat thing happen, and then learn the scientific explanation for the effect you experienced. For children too young to read the accompanying text, a friendly 'Explainer' is usually there to translate. (One of the museum's many educational initiatives –the Science Career Ladder – offers students the opportunity to work as Explainer; as a result, the museum is generally well-stocked with young enthusiastic staff.)

The outdoor Science Playground is the museum's crown jewel. An exceptionally innovative and colourful arena, it is packed with games at once educational and entertaining. Among the other crowd-pleasing activities available, visitors can direct sunbeams at light-activated kinetic sculpture, play with windmills and water, and climb on a giant

three-dimensional web of ropes. Another key attraction is the original 1964 Great Hall itself, which is accessible through the museum when travelling exhibitions are on display there. A serpentine building composed of a mosaic of cobalt glass and concrete, the Great Hall's interior is especially attractive on clear days when the sun shining through the brilliant blue glass creates a radiant, cathedral-like effect.

ADDRESS 47–01 111th Street, Flushing Meadows Corona Park, NY 11368; (718) 699 0005; www.nyhallsci.org
OPEN Monday to Wednesday, 9.30–14.00; Thursday to Sunday, 9.30–17.00 (July and August, Monday, 9.30–14.00; Tuesday to Sunday, 9.30–17.00). Playground open April to November for children aged 6 and older ($2 extra)
ADMISSION $7.50; seniors and children aged 4 to 17 $5; free for children under 4; free admission September to June, Thursday and Friday, 14.00–17.00
DISABILITY ACCESS full
SUBWAY 7 to 111th Street

PS1 Contemporary Art Center

In 1976, the abandoned Queens Public School 1 was converted into PS1 in order to create an alternative studio and exhibition space for artists then ignored by the city's museum establishment. On three sides, the nineteenth-century red-brick school building is perfectly congruous with the typical Queens neighbourhood that surrounds it. Enter within the massive concrete walls of the outdoor gallery that serves as the entrance, however, and you are hard pressed to remember that you are in Long Island City. This oscillation between the abstract 'world apart' of the art space and the particularity of its surroundings is reproduced throughout the museum in a deliberate refusal to draw the line between the interior of the museum's galleries and its infrastructure. Artworks by James Turrell and Julian Schnabel overlook the city from the roof. One installation literally thrusts the visitor outside the building to view the Manhattan skyline upside-down. Very often, visitors have access to installations as they are being mounted, and artists-in-residence are encouraged to open their studios to the public.

Site-specific pieces occupy PS1's hallways, stairwells, offices, and attic. This blurring of boundaries, however, is neither executed willy-nilly, nor proffered as an end in itself. It's not obvious why two important Robert Ryman paintings have been placed in the boiler room until you go down there and see how they work with the ambience of the dusty room and the illumination of a couple of skylights. Because the art spills over into unexpected places, it's easy to unwittingly bypass individual pieces. Don't miss Robert Wogan's 'Interior', which you have to pass through a darkened crawlspace on the top floor to get to. And, as you enter the lobby, turn left and look down to see Piplotti Rist's tiny 'Selbstlos im Lavabad': a video-image of the artist calls plaintively to you through a hole in the floor.

PS1 Contemporary Art Center

queens

PS1 Contemporary Art Center

As well as conserving long-term loans and traces of site-specific pieces from as far back as the museum's inception, PS1 is extremely responsive to new developments in art. If the institution's remarkable capacity to sustain a feeling of intimacy between artworks spread over 23 years and 125,000 square feet is due in part to its lack of red tape and permanent collections, it remains to be seen how PS1 will be affected by its recent merger with MOMA.

ADDRESS 22–25 Jackson Avenue (at 46th Avenue), Long Island City (Queens), NY 11101; (718) 784 2084; www.ps1.org
OPEN Wednesday to Sunday, 12.00–18.00
ADMISSION free
DISABILITY ACCESS limited
SUBWAY E, F at 23rd and Eli; 7 to 45th Road and Courthouse Square; G to 21st Street/Van Alst

Queens Museum of Art

In order to reach the QMA, follow your way out to that giant steel globe that juts out over Flushing. The 'Unisphere' is a remnant of the New York World's Fairs of 1939 and 1964, and so is the museum's building and much of its collection. The QMA was founded in 1972 for the purpose of maintaining the Panorama of the City of New York, a 9335 square-foot model of the city. Originally constructed for the 1964 World's Fair, the Panorama is the world's largest architectural scale model. Conceived by master builder and President of the 1964 New York World's Fair Corporation Robert Moses, the Panorama reflects the extensive impact that Moses had on the development of New York. 25,000 units were custom-made over two years to represent particular museums, churches, or skyscrapers. New Yorkers from all five boroughs can pick out their homes among the other 800,000 standardised units. Planes take off from La Guardia and land at JFK, and the lighting runs through a 24-hour cycle every 10 minutes.

The fate of the Panorama after the 1964 Fair closely follows the ups and downs of the city it represents. At one point, plans were made to break the model up and send each borough to its respective Borough Hall. Moses' intention of updating the Panorama annually (in order to use the model as an actual tool of urban planning) lapsed during the fiscal crises of the early 1970s. During the economic upturn of the 1980s, however, architects donated models of the massive structures going up in midtown. In 1992, the Panorama underwent extensive refurbishment, and opened to the public in 1994.

In adjacent galleries, the QMA displays an extensive collection of artefacts from both World's Fairs, including a 'helicopter ride' that lifted visitors over the Panorama in 1964 to marvel at the vast expanse of New York. Text, memorabilia, and photographs combine to reveal how

earnest, utopian, and surprisingly bawdy were these spectacular homages to development and technology.

Though the museum was originally founded solely for the purposes of maintaining the Panorama, it has recently evolved into an art museum as well. In juxtaposition with the Panorama, the 'A' in QMA makes the museum something of a hodge-podge. However, while the large spare gallery displaying plaster casts of classical and Renaissance sculpture on long-term loan from the Met is merely disorienting, the QMA's often international exhibitions of twentieth-century and contemporary art are usually intelligent and ambitious. As was the case with a recent show, 'Global Conceptualism: Points of Origin, 1950s–1980s', they occasionally provide unexpected connections and counter-points to the exhibits on the World's Fairs. The museum also displays an impressive collection of Tiffany glassware and lamps. The Panorama occasions lectures by architects, urban planners, and historians.

ADDRESS New York City Building, Flushing Meadows Corona Park, Queens, NY 11368; (718) 592 9700; www.queensmuse.org
OPEN Wednesday to Friday, 10.00–17.00; Saturday, Sunday, 12.00–17.00
ADMISSION $4; seniors, students, and children $2
DISABILITY ACCESS full
SUBWAY 7 (Flushing line) to Willets Point/Shea Stadium

staten island

Alice Austen House 11.2
Jacques Marchais Museum of Tibetan Art 11.6

Alice Austen House

This extremely quaint house was originally a Dutch farmhouse, dating back to around 1700. The house was converted to a Gothic Revival-style Victorian cottage and christened 'Clear Comfort' when it was bought by the Austens in 1844, and its exterior and grounds, as well as its parlour, have been restored to their nineteenth-century appearance with the aid of Alice Austen's photographs. Perched on a tiny hill overlooking the house's landscaped gardens, the New York skyline, and the Narrows – a scenic and busy shipping channel – the house is worth visiting for the view alone.

The museum is also interesting as an introduction to the fascinating life of Austen, one of the few nineteenth-century female documentary photographers whose work has been recognised and preserved. She started taking photographs at the age of 18 and produced thousands over the course of her life. Although many of her works depict what she called 'the larky life' – the privileged social activities that she participated in as a member of one of Staten Island's wealthier families – she also flouted conventions of feminine propriety, venturing into poverty-stricken neighbourhoods in Manhattan to take photographs of immigrant life and destitution. She never married, but lived instead with a female companion for 55 years before losing her wealth in the stock-market crash of 1929 and ending up in the city poorhouse. Though she had never tried to sell her work, it was finally discovered in her old age, and the proceeds from its sale enabled her to resettle in a retirement home before her death in 1952.

Be sure to watch the illuminating documentary video on Austen's life. Despite being slightly outmoded, it allows visitors to see a vast array of her photography and provides copious information about her life and social context. Once your interest in her has been piqued by the house

Alice Austen House

and the video, however, it comes as a disappointment that the museum only has a small selection of her photos on view. In fact, the vast majority of her work is retained by the Staten Island Historical Society in nearby Richmond Town. (Call (718) 351 1611 for an appointment to see their collection.)

ADDRESS 2 Nylan Boulevard (at Edgewater Street), Staten Island, NY 10305; (718) 816 4506
OPEN Thursday to Sunday, 12.00–17.00
ADMISSION $2
DISABILITY ACCESS full
SUBWAY 1, 9 to South Ferry; then take ferry to Staten Island; bus S51 to Hylan Boulevard

Jacques Marchais Museum of Tibetan Art

Given the relatively humble size of its collection, and the fact that most visitors will have to undergo a minor odyssey to reach its remote location, this museum will probably prove most rewarding to those with a specific interest in Tibetan art. Even a non-connoisseur, though, might be tempted to make the pilgrimage in order to visit the museum's lovely grounds. Designed to replicate the look and feel of a Tibetan mountain temple, the museum's location on a wooded hillside road offers lush green views of the surrounding valley. In warm weather, its stone sculptures, terraces and goldfish pond make it amenable to a meditative stroll or quiet picnic.

Jacqueline Klauber, a mid-Westerner with a passion for Tibetan art and culture, adopted the name Jacques Marchais in order to compete more effectively in the male-dominated art dealer's world of the earlier part of the century. In 1945, she began to construct the museum and its stone buildings on the current site on Staten Island, but died shortly before the museum was opened to the public in 1947. Like the exterior of the museum, the interior is meant to evoke a Tibetan temple. A significant portion of its eclectic array of art, including metal statues, *thangka* paintings and shrine furniture, has been arranged in the form of an altar, where the objects can be viewed by visitors in both their aesthetic and ceremonial functions. Dating from the seventeenth to nineteenth centuries, and even earlier in some cases, the collection also contains examples of jewel-encrusted Nepalese metalwork, silver ceremonial implements, masks, jewellery, and imperial Chinese cloisonné decorative objects.

The art's origins, (which include China, Mongolia and Nepal, as well as Tibet) and its significance are interpreted for visitors by a tour-guide and/or by a 20-minute video (both available on request). Flyers with staten island

11.8

information about individual aspects of the exhibition are stationed conveniently around the room. Among the many fascinating objects on view, the painstakingly crafted sand mandalas and the cups made out of human skulls are particularly worth noting.

The museum offers a number of educational programmes aimed at a wide variety of age-groups, including schoolchildren. Topics include Tibetan art and culture; symbols and hand gestures used in Tibetan art; the Dalai Lama; environmental problems in Tibet. Special programmes for the visually impaired are also available.

staten island

ADDRESS 338 Lighthouse Avenue, Staten Island, NY 10306; (718) 987 3500; www. tibetanmuseum.com
OPEN April to November, Wednesday to Sunday, 13.00–17.00; December to March, Wednesday to Friday, 13.00–17.00
ADMISSION $3; students and seniors $2.50; children under 12, $1
DISABILITY ACCESS none
BUS from Staten Island Ferry, take S74 to Lighthouse Avenue

index

Index

Abbott, Berenice 5.24
Abram, Ruth 1.10
Adams, John 5.2
African-American Wax and History Museum of Harlem **6.2–6.4**
African Art, see Museum for African Art 2.8
Albright, Madeleine 4.2
Alexander Hamilton US Custom House 1.24
Alice Austen House **11.2–11.4**
American Craft Museum **4.2**, 6.18
American Indian, see National Museum of the American Indian
American Museum of Natural History **6.6–6.8**
American Museum of the Moving Image **10.2–10.4**
American Numismatic Society 0.2, **7.2**
Americas Society **4.4**
AMMI, see American Museum of the Moving Image
Antiquities, see National Museum of the American Indian, Queens Museum of Art, Metropolitan Museum of Art, The Morgan Library
Arabic art, see Brooklyn Museum of Art
Arbus, Diane 5.24
Archipenko, Alexander 2.14
Asia Society 0.5, **5.6**
Astor, John Jacob 4.26
Audubon, John James 6.20
Audubon Terrace 0.2
Austen, Alice 11.2

Barnard, George Grey 7.6
Barnes, Edward Larrabee 5.6
Battery Park City 1.30
Bess Myerson Film and Video Collection 1.22
Beuys, Joseph 3.2
BMA, see Brooklyn Museum of Art
Brady, Matthew 6.20
Breuer, Marcel 5.40
Bronx County Historical Society 8.4
Bronx Museum of the Arts **8.2**
Brooklyn Bridge 9.6
Brooklyn Children's Museum 0.6, 6.14, **9.2–9.4**
Brooklyn Dodgers 9.6
Brooklyn Historical Society **9.6**
Brooklyn Museum of Art 0.1, 0.2, 0.5, **9.8–9.10**
Brooklyn Navy Yard 9.6
Burr, Aaron 7.14

Cafés and restaurants, see El Museo del Barrio, Fraunces Tavern Museum, The Jewish Museum, Metropolitan Museum of Art, The Morgan Library, The Museum of Modern Art
Calder, Alexander 5.42
Calle, Sophie 5.26
Capa, Cornell 5.24
Capa, Robert 5.24
Carrère and Hastings 0.2, 4.26, 5.16
Cartier-Bresson, Henri 5.24
Cathedral of St John the Divine **6.10–6.12**
Central Park 0.1

Ceramics, *see* Hispanic Society of America, Japan Society

Chagall, Marc 5.20

Chanticleer, Raven 6.2

Children, *see also* Brooklyn Children's Museum

Children's Museum of Manhattan (CMOM) 0.6, **6.14–6.16**

Children's Museum of the Native American **7.4**

Chilindron, Martha 5.12

Chinatown History Project 1.16

Church, Frederic E 5.8, 5.38

Civil War 0.1

Clemente, Francesco 3.2

The Cloisters **7.6**

Cole, Thomas 6.20

Coney Island 9.6

Contemporary art, *see* American Museum of the Moving Image, Bronx Museum of the Arts, Dia Center for the Arts, Metropolitan Museum, The Museum of Modern Art, PS1

Cooper, Peter 5.8

Cooper-Hewitt, National Design Museum **5.8–5.10**

Corona Park 10.8

Costumes, *see* The Kurdish Library and Museum, The Museum at Fashion Institute of Technology

Croft, Lara 10.2

Crown Heights 9.4

Curtis, Edward S 7.4

Delaunay, Robert 5.20

Design, *see* Cooper Hewitt, The Museum of Modern Art, National Design Museum, National Academy of Design

Detrich, Kalman 1.28

Dia Center for the Arts 0.4, **3.2–3.4**

Dinkins, David 6.2

Duveen, Joseph 5.16

Dyckman, William 7.8

Dyckman Farmhouse Museum **7.8**

Edgar Allan Poe Cottage **8.4**

Ellis Island Immigration Museum **1.2–1.4**

Emancipation Proclamation 2.2

Ethnic focus, *see* African-American Wax and History Museum of Harlem, Americas Society, Asia Society, Bronx Museum of the Arts, Children's Museum of the Native American, El Museo del Barrio, Hispanic Society of America, Jacques Marchais Museum of Tibetan Art, Japan Society, Museum for African Art, Museum of American Folk Art, Museum of Chinese in the Americas, Museum of Jewish Heritage, Museum of the American Indian, Museum of the City of New York, The Jewish Museum, The Kurdish Library and Museum, The Schomburg Center for Research in Black Culture, The Studio Museum in Harlem, The Ukrainian Museum

Fabergé eggs 2.2

Film and video, *see* American Museum of the Moving Image, The Museum of

Index

Jewish Heritage, The Kurdish Library and Museum
Fisher, Zachary 4.6
FIT, see The Museum at Fashion Institute of Technology
Flavin, Dan 3.2
Flushing Meadows Corona Park 10.10, 10.18
Forbes Magazine Galleries 0.6, **2.2**
Fort Tryon Park 7.6
Fraunces Tavern Museum **1.6–1.8**
The Frick Collection 0.2, **5.16–5.18**, 7.10
Frick, Henry Clay 5.16
Fry, Roger 5.16
Fulton Fish Market 1.32
Furniture and design, modern, see American Craft Museum, Museum of Modern Art, National Academy of Design

Gehry, Frank O 5.22
George Gustav Haye Center 1.24
Gilbert, Cass 1.24
Graham, Dan 3.2
Graham, Martha 10.6
Greenwich Village 2.4
Griffith, D W 4.16
Solomon R Guggenheim Museum 0.4, **5.20–5.22**

Haring, Keith 6.10
Hastings, Thomas 5.16
Heckscher Building 5.12
Heckscher Theater 5.14
Hewitt, Eleanor and Sarah 5.8

Hispanic Society of America **7.10–7.12**
Historic homes and period furnishings, see Alice Austen House, Dyckman Farmhouse Museum, Edgar Allan Poe Cottage, Fraunces Tavern Museum, The Frick Collection, Merchant's House Museum, Morris-Jumel Mansion, The Mount Vernon Hotel Museum and Garden
History, see Bronx County Historical Society, Brooklyn Historical Society, Chinatown History Project, Hispanic Society of America, New York Historical Society, Staten Island Historical Society
Holzer, Jenny 3.2
Homer, Winslow 5.8
Hopper, Edward 5.42
Hunt, Richard Morris 5.30
Huntington, Archer Milton 7.10

International Center of Photography 0.4, **5.24**
Intrepid Sea Air Space Museum **4.6–4.8**
The Isamu Noguchi Garden Museum **10.6**

Jacques Marchais Museum of Tibetan Art **11.6–11.8**
James, Henry 2.4
Japan Society **4.10**
The Jewish Museum **5.26–5.28**
Jiménez, Juan-Ramón 7.10
Johns, Jasper 5.40
Johnson, Jonathan Eastman 5.38

Johnson, Magic 6.2
Johnson, Philip 4.18, 4.20
Jumel, Stephen and Eliza 7.14

Kalman, Maira 6.14
Kandinsky, Vassily 5.20
Kensett, John Frederick 5.38
Klauber, Jacqueline, see Marchais, Jacques
The Kurdish Library and Museum **9.12**
Kurosawa, Kisho 4.10

Lady Day (Billie Holliday) 6.2
Léger, Ferdinand 5.20
Lennon, John 6.14
Lenox, James 4.26
Lewis, Norman 7.18
Lin, Maya 2.8
Long Island Historical Society, see Brooklyn Historical Society
Lower East Side Tenement Museum **1.10**–**1.12**

McKim, Charles 9.8
McKim, Mead & White 0.2, 4.4, 4.12, 5.30, 6.20
Marchais, Jacques 11.6
Marden, Brice 3.2
Marine interest, see Intrepid Sea Air Space Museum
Meier, Richard 4.22
Merchant's House Museum **2.4**–**2.6**
Metropolitan Museum of Art 0.1, 0.2, **5.30**–**5.32**
Military interest, see Intrepid Sea Air Space Museum
MOCA, see Museum of Chinese in the Americas
Modern art, see Dia Center for the Arts, Metropolitan Museum of Art, Solomon R Guggenheim Museum, Museum of Modern Art, PS1, The Studio Museum in Harlem, Whitney Museum of American Art
MOMA, see The Museum of Modern Art
The Morgan Library **4.12**–**4.14**, 7.10
Mori, Mariko 4.10, 9.10
Morris, Roger 7.14
Morris-Jumel Mansion 5.2, **7.14**–**7.16**
Morse, Samuel F B 5.38
Moses, Robert 10.16
The Mount Vernon Hotel Museum and Garden **5.2**–**5.4**
Municipal Archives of the City of New York **1.14**
Musée des Arts Décoratifs 5.8
El Museo del Barrio **5.12**–**5.14**
The Museum of Modern Art (MOMA) 0.3, 0.4, **4.16**–**4.18**, 6.18
The Museum at Fashion Institute of Technology (FIT) 0.4, **3.6**
Museum for African Art **2.8**–**2.10**
Museum Mile 5.12, 5.24
Museum of American Folk Art 4.2, **6.18**
Museum of Chinese in the Americas (MOCA) 0.5, **1.16**–**1.18**
Museum of Jewish Heritage **1.20**–**1.22**
Museum of Natural History 0.1, 0.2, 0.3
Museum of the American Indian 0.3
Museum of the American Piano **1.28**

Index

Museum of the City of New York 0.3, **5.34–5.36**
Museum of TV & Radio 0.4, **4.20–4.22**
Muybridge, Eadweard 5.24

National Academy of Design 0.2, 0.6, **5.38**
National Museum of the American Indian 0.3, **1.24–1.26**
Newman, Barnett 3.2
Newseum/NY **4.24**
New York, museums about, *see* Brooklyn Historical Society, Brooklyn Museum, Brooklyn Museum of Art, Ellis Island Immigration Museum, Lower East Side Tenement Museum, Museum of the City of New York, Municipal Archives of the City of New York, South Street Seaport Museum
New York Botanical Garden 8.4
New York City Ballet 6.20
New York City Fire Museum **2.12**
New York City Oyster Festival 2.6
New York Hall of Science **10.8–10.10**
New York Historical Society 0.1, **6.20**
New York Police Department 6.20
New York Public Library 0.2, **4.26–4.28**
New York Transit Museum **9.14**
New York World's Fair 5.2
Noguchi, Isamu 10.6

O'Keefe, Georgia 5.42
Outdoor space, *see* Central Park, Children's Museum of Manhattan, The Cloisters, Morris-Jumel Mansion, The Studio Museum in Harlem

Palermo, Blinky 3.2
Paley, William S 4.20
Panorama of the City of New York 10.16
Photography, *see* International Center of Photography
Pollock, Jackson 5.20
Post, George B 9.6
PS1 Contemporary Art Center 0.4, 0.5, **10.12–10.14**
Pysanky 2.14

Queens Museum of Art **10.16–10.18**

Rare books and manuscripts, *see* The Morgan Library, New York Public Library
Richter, Gerhard 3.2
Rist, Piplotti 10.12
Rockefeller III, John D 4.10
Rockefeller Jr, John D 7.6
Rodin, August 9.8
Rogers, Jacob S 0.1
Roosevelt, Theodore 2.2
Rothko, Mark 5.20
Rukeyser, Muriel 6.10
Ryder, Albert Pinkham 9.10
Ryman, Robert 3.2, 10.12

Sadao, Shoji 10.6
Saint John the Divine, see Cathedral of St John the Divine
Sánchez, Juan 5.12
Schnabel, Julian 10.12

The Schomburg Center for Research in
   Black Culture 4.26
Sculpture 10.6
The Shadow 4.20
Sherman, Cindy 5.40
The Skyscraper Museum **1.30**
Smith, Abigail Adams 5.2
Smith, Colonel William Stephens 5.2
Smith, Hamilton 5.40
Smithsonian 1.24, 5.8
South Street Seaport Museum **1.32**
Star Trek 4.20
Staten Island Historical Society 11.4
Streets, etc
   12th Street 2.2
   27th Street 3.6
   36th Street 10.4
   42nd Street 4.28
   43rd Street 5.24
   56th Street 4.24
   57th Street 4.24
   70th Street 5.6
   75th Street 5.42
   79th Street 6.8
   82nd Street 5.32
   89th Street 5.22, 5.38
   94th Street 5.24
   103rd Street 5.36
   104th Street 5.14
   111th Street 10.10
   112th Street 6.12
   155th Street 7.2
   160th Street 7.16
   162nd Street 7.16
   204th Street 7.8

Amsterdam Avenue 6.12
Audubon Terrace 7.2, 7.12
Avenue of the Americas 5.24
Bayard Street 1.18
Boerum Place (Brooklyn) 9.14
The Bowery 2.6
Bowling Green 1.26
Broad Street 1.8
Broadway 1.28, 2.10, 7.2, 7.8, 7.12
Brooklyn Avenue (Brooklyn) 9.4
Broome Street 1.12
Central Park West 6.8, 6.20
Chambers Street 1.14
East 36th Street 4.14
East 46th Street 4.30
East 47th Street 4.10
East 61st Street 5.4
East 70th Street 5.18
East 91st Street 5.10
Eastern Parkway (Brooklyn) 9.10
East Fourth Street 2.6
East Kingsbridge Road (Bronx) 8.4
Edgewater Street (Staten Island) 11.4
Eleventh Avenue 3.4
Fifth Avenue 2.2, 4.2, 4.18, 4.22, 4.28,
   5.10, 5.14, 5.18, 5.22, 5.24, 5.28,
   5.32, 5.36, 5.38
First Avenue 4.30, 5.4
First Place 1.22
Forty-sixth Avenue (Long Island) 10.14
Frederick Douglass Boulevard 6.4
Fulton Street 1.32
Grand Concourse (Bronx) 8.2, 8.4
Houston 2.10
Hudson 2.12

Index

Hylan Boulevard (Staten Island) 11.4
Jackson Avenue (Queens) 10.14
Jumel Terrace 7.16
Lafayette Street 2.6
Lenox Avenue 7.18
Lighthouse Avenue (Staten Island) 11.8
Lincoln Square 6.18
Madison Avenue 4.24, 5.42
Maiden Lane 1.30
Malcolm X Boulevard 4.28
Manhattan Avenue 6.4
Mulberry Street 1.18
New York Harbor 1.4
Orchard Street 1.12
Park Avenue 4.4, 5.6
Pearl Street 1.8
Pierrepont Street (Brooklyn) 9.6
Prince Street 2.10
Schermerhorn Street (Brooklyn) 9.14
Second Avenue 2.14
Seventh Avenue 3.6, 7.18
Sixth Avenue 4.2, 4.18, 4.22, 5.24
Spring Street 2.12
Thirty-fifth Avenue (Astoria) 10.4
Twelfth Avenue 4.8
Underhill Avenue (Brooklyn) 9.12
Varick 2.12
Vernon Boulevard (Queens) 10.6
West 22nd Street 3.4
West 46th Street 4.8
West 52nd Street 4.22
West 53rd Street 4.2, 4.18
West 77th Street 6.20
West 83rd Street 6.16
West 115th Street 6.4

West 125th Street 7.18
West 155th Street 7.4, 7.12
Wooster Street 3.4
York Avenue 5.4
The Studio Museum in Harlem **7.18**

Taniguchi, Yoshio 4.18
Textiles, *see* The Cloisters
Tubman, Harriet 6.2
Turrell, James 10.12
Twombly, Cy 3.2

The Ukrainian Museum **2.14**
United Nations **4.30**

Van Gogh, Vincent 4.16
Vespucci, Juan 7.12

Warhol, Andy 3.2, 4.16, 5.22
Washington, George 6.20, 7.14
Weber, Max 5.26
Weegee 5.24
Weiner, Lawrence 3.2
Wharton, Edith 5.30
Whitney, Gertrude Vanderbilt 5.40
Whitney Museum of American Art 0.3,
0.4, **5.40–5.42**
Williams, Robin 4.20
Wogan, Robert 10.12
WPA Federal Writers' Project 1.14
Wright, Frank Lloyd 5.20, 5.30

Yoshimura, Junzo 4.10

Photographs are by Simon Alexander except:

pages 1.5, 1.7 courtesy Fraunces Tavern Museum

pages 2.9, 2.11 courtesy Museum for African Art

pages 3.3 photo by Cathy Carmen; 3.5 photo by Todd Schroeder; courtesy Dia Center for the Arts

page 3.7 courtesy The Museum at Fashion Institute of Technology

page 4.3 courtesy American Craft Museum

page 4.5 photo by Lawrence Beck, courtesy Americas Society

page 5.7 courtesy Asia Society

page 5.9 photo by Andrew Garn, courtesy Cooper-Hewitt, National Design Museum, Smithsonian Institution

pages 5.17, 5.18, 5.19 courtesy The Frick Collection

pages 5.21, 5.23, courtesy Solomon R Guggenheim Museum

page 5.33 courtesy Metropolitan Museum of Art

pages 6.15, 6.17 courtesy Children's Museum of Manhattan

page 7.11 courtesy Hispanic Society of America

page 8.3 courtesy Bronx Museum of the Arts

page 10.7 courtesy The Isamu Noguchi Garden Museum

pages 10.13, 10.15 courtesy PS1 Contemporary Art Center